STAAR Prep
Grade 5
Reading Comprehension
Third Edition

by Mark Lyons

Item Code RAS 2585 • Copyright © 2013 Queue, Inc.

Queue, Inc. • 80 Hathaway Drive, Stratford, CT 06615
(800) 232-2224 • Fax: (800) 775-2729 • www.qworkbooks.com

Table of Contents

Read the article "A Day of Artistic Endeavors" before answering the questions below.

FLORENCE WEEKLY GAZETTE
Serving the Central Texas Community

May 17, 2012   **Section B**

A Day of Artistic Endeavors

1   The Florence High School hallways and courtyard were filled with art, drama, poetry, and music on Saturday, May 12. Students from the elementary school, middle school, and high school showed off their artistic skills with numerous displays scattered throughout the bright hallways of the high school. The Florence Fine Arts Festival began at 10:00 am and ran until 3:00 pm. Music groups performed all throughout the festival. Bands from the elementary, middle, and high schools performed various selections in the courtyard. Parents, visitors, and guests listened to works by Beethoven, Mozart, Copland, Sousa, and Stravinsky. Other, more modern pieces were also performed.

2   Ms. Nancy Griffin, the director of the high school band and the organizer of the event, was pleased with the performances of all of the bands. "I think everyone did an outstanding job," said Ms. Griffin. "The elementary band, directed by Mr. Mark Wheeling, sounded great. The middle school band, directed by Mr. Sam Waters, outdid themselves. My band was on their toes today. I don't think I have ever heard them play better. We are recording all of the performances today and a CD will be available next month. Pictures of each of the bands will also be ready at the same time."

3   Each band performed several times throughout the festival. Audience members were able to enjoy refreshments provided by the band booster parent organization. Funds raised from the sale of refreshments will go toward the purchase of additional instruments for the bands.

4   Inside the high school, art displays were set up along the walls and on long tables. Wildly decorated masks, colorful paintings, detailed drawings, sculptures, mobiles, and many other types of art were visible all through the <u>adjoining</u> halls of the high school. Name tags next to each display told the name and school of the artist. Proud parents and students wandered from one hall to the next, carefully taking in each piece.

5   The drama department of the high school presented three short plays during the festival. Audience members were able to watch each performance in the high school auditorium. Bright lights lit up the stage. Colorful costumes and scenery helped tell the stories of the three plays. Each play was met with excitement and a great deal of applause.

6   Ms. Barbara Joyner, the high school drama teacher, said, "I am so proud of each of the actors, stage crew members, and behind-the-scenes students. They all worked together. Each play went off without a hitch. We look forward to doing this again next year."

7   Various students from all three schools read poems throughout the day. Individuals, as well as small and large groups presented poems by many different poets.

8   Parents, students, and teachers were all impressed with the festival. A parent, Mr. Robert Smith, said, "My daughter has been practicing and looking forward to today for over three months. I know these pieces of music so well that I think I could play along. Her band did an outstanding job. I enjoyed listening to every selection."

9   Ms. Maxine Johnson, a math teacher at the middle school, had this to say about the play that she saw: "I remember performing that same play when I was in high school many years ago. The performance these kids did today was awesome."

10 Natalie Warren, a student at the elementary school, said, "I am going to try out for band next year. I really liked the trumpets when I heard the middle school band play. They were great. Every note was loud and clear."

11 Saturday's festival was the first one to be held in Florence. Ms. Griffin said that plans are already underway for next year's fine arts festival. "It is a lot of hard work, but seeing the joy and excitement on these kids' faces makes it all worth it."

12 A survey about the festival was taken. Those who attended the festival were asked about their favorite part of the event. Results are shown in the graph on the following page.

2

Favorite Events at Florence Fine Arts Festival

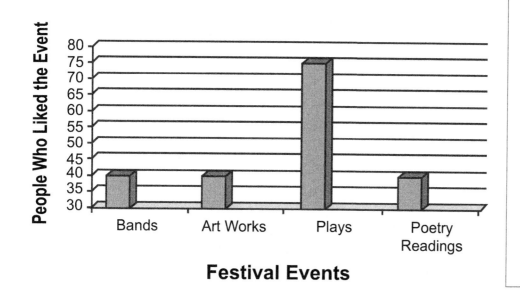

My Notes About What I Am Reading

(Category 1 – 2 B – RS)

1. In paragraph 4, the word <u>adjoining</u> means

   A   next to.

   B   same as.

   C   generous.

   D   excellent.

(Category 3 – 11 A – RS)

2. This article is mostly about the

   A   Florence public schools.

   B   process of playing a musical instrument.

   C   Florence Fine Arts Festival.

   D   planning of a band festival

(Category 3 – Figure 19 D – RS)

3. The reader can tell that the band students' parents

    A   wish they could play along.

    B   support the bands at the schools.

    C   spend a lot of money at the festival.

    D   are concerned about the bands practicing too much.

(Category 3 – 11 B – SS)

4. Which of these sentences from the article expresses a fact?

    A   *Every note was loud and clear.*

    B   *It is a lot of hard work, but seeing the joy and excitement on these kids' faces makes it all worth it.*

    C   *Each play was met with excitement and a great deal of applause.*

    D   *The drama department of the high school presented three short plays during the festival.*

(Category 3 – 13 A – SS)

5. From information provided in the graph, the reader can tell that

    A   more people liked to listen to music than liked to see art work.

    B   fewer people liked poems than liked plays.

    C   more people enjoyed art work than liked poetry.

    D   less people enjoyed plays than enjoyed music.

Read this selection. Then answer the questions that follow it.

THE BIKE MAN

1   Brandon rode slowly past the old yellow house that sat behind four tall oak trees at the end of his block. A tall shabby barn, in desperate need of fresh paint, loomed next to the house. Ever since Brandon and his family had moved into their new home, he had wondered about this house. He knew an elderly man, Mr. Micah Samuels, owned the house, barn, and the 100 acres that surrounded them. It blocked the path of newly constructed streets and homes.

2   Mr. Samuels refused to sell to developers and spent his days tinkering in a back room of the old barn. Brandon's friends told him to stay away from Mr. Samuels. Even though nothing had happened, they all seemed fearful of him, including Brandon. Up until now, Brandon had never had any dealings with Mr. Samuels. Brandon often saw Mr. Samuels loading things into the back of his old, rusting pickup truck, but it was either too dark or too far away for Brandon to see the contents.

3   Standing on his pedals, Brandon coasted next to the curb in front of Mr. Samuel's house and peered intently into the open barn door. As always, the pickup was backed into the barn and Mr. Samuels was putting another load onto the truck. Brandon wheeled his bicycle around and waited across the street, determined to catch a glimpse in the truck if it drove by before he had to be home.

4   After about an hour, the light began to fade as sunset drew near. Brandon had to get home. As he pushed off from the curb, the truck's engine roared to life. Twin beams of light pierced the settling darkness as the noisy pickup rattled out of the barn toward the street. Brandon quickly turned around just in time to see the bed of the pickup roll, covered by a dusty gray tarp. No luck again.

5   After school the next day, as Brandon prepared to deliver newspapers to the customers on his paper route, he was surprised to see his father's car pull into the driveway. His dad rarely got home this early. Sensing something was wrong, Brandon walked into the kitchen just as he heard his dad talking to his mom.

6   "Helen, my department has been cut back," said Mr. Davis. "I've been laid off for at least six months. The company promises they will rehire us again come September, if not before. We are going to have to cut back around here and pinch pennies until then. Maybe I can get a temporary job down at the mill. I know the fore-

5

man from high school."

7   "Dad, is everything okay?" asked Brandon.

8   "No, son, it is not. We will make it though, as long as we don't have to spend extra. Money is going to be very tight around here for the next couple of months. There is enough money in our savings account for a while. I should be hired back before we run out. If not, I will get another job somewhere else," replied Mr. Davis as he hugged his wife and son.

9   "You better get on with your deliveries, Brandon," said Mr. Davis as he wiped his eyes. "You have people waiting for their afternoon paper."

10 Brandon had never pedaled so fast. He didn't quite know what to think. His mind was as full of thoughts as a pot of overflowing popping corn. He blindly hurried from house to house on his route. Usually he liked working alone on his route, but today he just wanted to get home.

11 The last person getting a paper lived on the fourth floor of a small apartment building near his home. Brandon always locked his bicycle to the lamppost outside of the building before he went upstairs to deliver the paper. But this time, with all that he had on his mind, Brandon just set the bicycle up against the post and rushed upstairs. He was gone for only a few minutes, but when he returned, his bicycle was on where in sight.

12 "Oh, no! My bike's been stolen!" hollered Brandon.

13 He rushed up and down the sidewalk looking for his bike, but to no avail. It was no where to be found.

14 "What else is going to happen today?" he muttered to himself as he trudged home. When he got home, Brandon explained to his parents what had happened. Relieved that he was safe, Brandon's mom gave him a comforting hug.

15 "I don't want you walking to school and home again," she said. "I will pick you up and your dad will take you.

16 "I'd pick you up too, but I just got off of the telephone with the mill foreman and he hired me part time. I start tomorrow," added his dad. "What are you going to do about your paper route?"

17 "I'll ask Daniel from across the street if I can borrow his bike. If not, I will have to walk the route, I guess," answered Brandon. "I probably won't get home until late, but I don't want my customers to complain. I will do what it takes. I don't want to lose this job."

My Notes About What I Am Reading

6

18 The next day, Brandon asked Daniel if he could borrow his bike. Daniel agreed, but only for a few days. Baseball practice was starting and he needed it to get to the ball fields after school and help the coach get set up.

19 After school, Brandon rolled all of his newspapers, stuck them into two bags, threw the bags over his shoulders, and set off from his front porch to walk his paper route. As he turned onto the sidewalk in front of his house, he heard the rattle of a vehicle approach and slow to a stop. Glancing over, Brandon saw that it was an old rusting pickup. Climbing out of the cab was the tall figure of Mr. Samuels. Brandon hesitated, not sure of what to expect. Without saying a word, Mr. Samuels walked to the rear of the truck and pulled back the tarp. Brandon was surprised to see shiny bicycles of all shapes and sizes lined neatly in a row. Reaching in, Mr. Samuels grabbed a blue single speed bicycle, hefted it over the side of the pickup and down onto the sidewalk next to Brandon.

20 "Here son," said Mr. Samuels standing next to the bicycle. "I heard about your troubles. This is what I do. I fix up old bicycles and give them to those who need them. All that I ask is that you help me find other people in need of a bike, too.

21 Brandon was speechless. Now he understood about all of the times that he had seen Mr. Samuels <u>consistently</u> working in his barn and loading stuff into the back of his pickup.

22 Mr. Samuels held out his hand. Daniel shook it and felt the rough, calluses of a fine craftsman.

23 "Mr. Samuels, I would be honored to help. Thank you so much," Brandon said.

24 "Okay, son," grinned Mr. Samuels. "But you better get moving. You have some newspaper customers in need of their papers."

(Category 1 – 2 B – RS)

1. In paragraph 21, the word <u>consistently</u> means

    A   carelessly.
    B   noisily.
    C   regularly.
    D   skillfully.

(Category 2 – 6 A – RS)

2. Which conflict in the passage is resolved in paragraphs 19 through 24?

    A   Brandon will be late for school.
    B   Mr. Samuels needs a new pickup truck.
    C   Mr. Davis loses his job.
    D   Brandon will have a difficult time delivering newspapers.

(Category 2 – 6 B – RS)

3. How does Brandon change one of his relationships in the story?

    A   He finds that Mr. Samuels is a nice man.
    B   He wants to help the coach with the baseball team.
    C   He decides to help his dad find a job.
    D   He realizes his newspaper customers need their papers delivered on time.

8

(Category 2 – 8 A – RS)

4. The author's use of figurative language in paragraph 10 emphasizes that

    A   Brandon feels overwhelmed by his situation.
    B   Brandon wants to get home so he can eat.
    C   Brandon is angry about his father losing his job.
    D   Brandon worries that he will be late delivering newspapers.

(Category 2 – Figure 19 D – RS)

5. The reader can conclude that Brandon

    A   is willing to work hard.
    B   isn't good at delivering papers.
    C   isn't used to working alone.
    D   has delivered papers on foot before.

(Category 2 – 6 C – SS)

6. The reader can conclude that the passage "The Bike Man" is written from the third person point of view because

    A   Mr. Samuels tells the story.
    B   Brandon tells the story.
    C   Someone other than a character in the story tells the story.
    D   Mr. Davis tells the story.

(Category 2 – Figure 19 D – RS)

7. Which sentence from the story shows that Brandon does not give up easily?

   A   *"I'll do what it takes."*
   B   *"Dad, is everything okay?"*
   C   *"What else is going to happen today?"*
   D   *"Mr. Samuels, I would be honored to help."*

(Category 2 – Figure 19 E – RS)

8. Read the first sentence of a summary of the story.

   > **Summary of "The Bike Man"**
   >
   > Brandon watches Mr. Samuels and wonders what he loads into his pickup truck. _____
   > _____

Which set of sentences best completes the summary?

   A   Brandon waits to see what is in the back of the truck. He waits, but the truck drives away too fast. Brandon finds out later that Mr. Samuels repairs bicycles.
   B   Brandon is a little afraid of Mr. Samuels. Mr. Samuels lives at the end of Brandon's street. Brandon sits on his bicycle and tries to look in the back of the truck as it drives by.
   C   Then Brandon's father is laid off from his job and Brandon's bike is stolen while he is delivering newspapers. Mr. Samuels comes by and gives Brandon a bicycle.
   D   Then Brandon has to deliver newspapers to people in town. His bicycle gets taken and Brandon has to borrow Daniel's bike for a few days.

Read the next two selections, "Cowboy Wilbur" and "Ranching Today", before answering the questions below.

COWBOY WILBUR

1   "Yippee ki ya ki yo!" hollered Cowboy Wilbur as he waved his twenty-gallon hat high over his flowing golden locks. "Git along little deeries…I mean doggies!" He was always getting the cows mixed up with deer. It was the horns that threw him off.

2   Cowboy Wilbur stretched tall in the saddle. He loved this time of day out on the trail. Gentle winds blew in his face. Flies buzzed in and out of his ears. The glow of the sun reached just over the far horizon, showering the countryside with its soft pink light. The cattle slowly lumbered toward the river where they would cross over on their way up to the high pasture.

3   "Hey, little spotted deer…er, calf! Yeah, you there with the tail!" yelled Cowboy Wilbur. "Don't linger behind! Stay up with the rest of us!" He grabbed his trusty lariat, ready for action, but the calf caught up.

4   Cowboy Wilbur was good with his lariat. C.W. was lightning quick and had deadly <u>accuracy</u>. He could rope a mosquito's left wing at one hundred paces and not even work up a sweat.

5   Once, Cowboy Wilbur had rescued a calf with "Old Trusty" (that's what he called his lariat). It had wandered off during a fierce thunderstorm. C. W. found it on a high piece of land that was rapidly being swallowed by a flash flood. Cowboy Wilbur whipped out Old Trusty, twirled it over his head twice, and hurled the soaked rope across the raging waters. Snagging the frightened animal, C. W. tied off his end of the rope around a sturdy oak tree. Then, as the waters swirled around the bawling cow, Cowboy Wilbur calmly and tirelessly hauled it to safety on his side of the swollen creek.

6   As the river drew closer, Cowboy Wilbur thought back on his morning so far. Up while the sun was still dreaming, C. W. had already repaired the corral fence, chopped firewood, plowed the north forty acres for wheat, and written a note to his grammy thanking her for the fluffy bunny slippers she had sent him for his birthday.

     11

7   The cattle knew the way to the river. They crossed at one spot all of the time so they wouldn't disturb the rest of the plants and animals that called the river home. The cattle forded the river with only one problem, some of the calves were afraid to go in the swift-moving water. C. W. ended up carrying all six of them across on his back. Once on the other side, it was just a hop, skip, and a jump up to the high pasture.

8   Familiar surroundings spurred the herd of cattle on to the wide lush pasture boxed in by three tall mountains. As the herd settled in, Cowboy Wilbur set to work putting up a wire fence along the open end of the high pasture. With the fence in place, C. W. would not have to worry about any of the cattle straying from the rest of the herd.

9   It took Cowboy Wilbur a little over four hours to set the wooden fence posts every 20 feet. He strung five rows of silver wire from one pole to the next along the mile wide stretch of land.

10   "I'm getting slow," C. W. muttered to himself. "Last year it only took me three hours to fence in the whole north 40. I better get more sleep at night."

11   Before he knew it, the sun was heading behind the mountains. Cowboy Wilbur left the herd and quietly rode through the newly-installed gate and back down to his ranch house. He would leave the herd at the high pasture for a few days before moving it to another pasture on the ranch. This helped the grass stay healthy and grow thicker.

12   Cowboy Wilbur thought about the round-up coming in a couple of weeks. He whistled and hummed an old cowboy song. He knew it would be a busy time, but the new calves needed to be branded. Besides, all of his friends and neighbors from nearby ranches and farms would be there to help.

13   "Come on, Stanley," C. W. hollered out loud to his faithful horse. "Let's get home before the sun goes down today. I want to read the last chapter of Cowboy Hank: Super Cowboy of the Western Plains to see if he rescues little Timmy from the well, and then I want to get to bed early."

12

RANCHING TODAY

1   Modern ranches raise beef cattle. The ranchers work hard every day to make sure that their cattle are healthy. They also take care of their land so it is productive and protected.

2   Cattle ranches rely on lots of green grass and fresh water to raise their cattle. Ranchers have learned over the years that these are two keys to having a successful ranch.

3   On many ranches, the cattle spend their time in pastures full of range grass. Bordered by fences, they will spend a couple of days in one pasture before moving on to another one. This constant moving helps the grass grow and also keeps the weeds from taking over. Rotating from one pasture to another helps keep the grasslands healthy and ready to support the herds of cattle for years to come.

4   Ranchers also make sure that the cattle have plenty of fresh water. Many ranchers drill wells to provide water to big holding tanks throughout their ranches. This protects nearby rivers or streams from the cattle herd. The cattle can't trample the banks and harm the delicate plant and animal habitat found along these areas.

5   Cattle and many different kinds of wild animals live together on a ranch. Wildlife have an opportunity to live well on the abundant grasslands found on many western ranches.

6   Every spring, most ranches have a round-up. Round-ups have been taking place for several hundred years. The cattle are rounded up so that the new calves can be branded and given shots to help keep them healthy. Friends and neighbors from nearby ranches will come and help.

7   Once the cows are all together, the ranchers separate the calves from their mothers. The calves are roped by cowboys on horseback and taken to the branding fire. The calves are branded to make them easy to identify. A hot piece of metal made into a special symbol of the ranch is heated over a fire and pressed against the side of each calf. It leaves an impression of the symbol on the calf that will remain for the rest of its life. The calves are also given shots to keep them protected from diseases.

8   Ranches range in size from a few hundred cattle to many thousands. Some farms have just a couple of cows. They all share the same goal. Ranchers want to raise healthy cattle while at the same time preserving the land and water for their cattle and the wide variety of wildlife that inhabit the land.

13

Use "Cowboy Wilbur" to answer questions 1 – 4.

(Category 1 – 2 B – RS)

1. In paragraph 4, the word <u>accuracy</u> means

    A   hitting what is aimed at.

    B   knowledge of a skill.

    C   answers to a problem.

    D   understanding of mistakes.

(Category 2 – Figure 19 E – RS)

2. Which is the best summary of this passage?

    A   ... Cowboy Wilbur takes his herd of cattle out early in the morning. He gets them across the river and then puts up a fence to keep them safe. C. W. heads back home at the end of the day.

    B   Cowboy Wilbur likes the early morning hours. He gets up early to work on chores at the ranch. He rescues some cows from a flash flood and takes some cattle up to the high pasture.

    C   Early morning chores keep Cowboy Wilbur busy. He saves some cows from a raging river. C. W. tries to keep his heard safe.

    D   Many chores keep Cowboy Wilbur busy all morning. He leads his cattle up to the high pasture. Cowboy Wilbur gets ready to round up the calves to get them branded.

(Category 2 – Figure 19 D – RS)

3. Which sentence from the story shows that Cowboy Wilbur is a caring person?

    A   *It took Cowboy Wilbur a little over four hours to set the wooden fence posts every 20 feet.*

    B   *Some of the calves were afraid to go in the swift moving water so C.W. ended up carrying all six of them across on his back.*

    C   *As the herd settled in, C. W. set to work putting up a wire fence along the open end of the high pasture.*

    D   *Cowboy Wilbur left the herd and quietly rode through the newly installed gate and back down to his ranch house.*

(Category 2 – 14 C – SS)

4. The picture is most likely included with "Cowboy Wilbur" to support the idea that

    A   horses are difficult to ride.
    B   Cowboy Wilbur has worked long hours in the saddle.
    C   Cowboy Wilbur is a gifted lariat thrower.
    D   saddles help keep a rider from falling off of a horse.

Use "Ranching Today" to answer questions 5 – 9.

(Category 3 – 11 A – RS)

5. What is the main idea of the passage?

    A   What a spring cattle round-up is
    B   How modern ranchers take care of cattle
    C   Why ranchers need to give shots to cattle
    D   How to raise cattle for food

(Category 1 – 2 A – RS)

6. In paragraph 3, the word <u>rotating</u> means

    A   leading.
    B   trading.
    C   sorting.
    D   moving.

15

(Category 3 – 10 A – SS)

7. What can the reader tell about cattle ranches from information in "Ranching Today"?

    A Ranches raise other animals besides cattle.
    B Cattle ranches are larger than farms.
    C Cattle ranches take a lot of work to run.
    D Cattle ranches are only concerned with raising healthy cattle.

(Category 3 – 11 C – RS)

8. During spring round-up, calves are roped by cowboys to

    A protect them from other cattle.
    B get them ready to be branded.
    C keep them away from the branding fires.
    D make sure they are not left behind.

(Category 3 – Figure 19 E – RS)

9. Which is the best summary of this passage?

    A Ranches raise beef cattle with green grass and fresh water. Cattle are moved from pasture to pasture to help keep the land and water protected. Ranches hold a round-up each spring to brand their cattle and protect the cattle from diseases.
    B Ranches can have a few hundred cattle to many thousands. Some ranches have only a few cows. The ranches use fences to help keep the cattle from getting away.
    C Cows like to eat grass and drink water. Ranches raise cattle by letting the cattle eat and drink. Many ranches drill their own wells to provide water.
    D Cows are kept safe from many diseases by getting shots. Ranches hold round-ups each year to help protect cattle from getting diseases. The round-ups give the ranches time to do this in the spring.

16

Use "Cowboy Wilbur" and "Ranching Today" to answer questions 10 and 11.

(Category 1 – Figure 19 F – RS)

10. An idea present in both selections is the

    A   need to protect cattle from diseases.
    B   hard work involved in putting up fences.
    C   dangers of flash floods after rainstorms.
    D   care taken to make sure the grass stays healthy.

(Category 3 – 11 E – RS)

11. One way these selections are alike is that both mention

    A   reading books for enjoyment.
    B   friends working together to help each other.
    C   the size of ranches.
    D   where ranches are located.

Read the article "Gliders" before answering the questions below.

GLIDERS

Into the Air

1   People have wanted to fly for hundreds of years. Many early attempts at flight tried to <u>mimic</u> how birds fly. These were not successful. Nevertheless, people continued to dream of one day flying through the air like a bird.

2   In the late 1700s, people finally made it off of the ground. Hot air powered the first lighter-than-air craft and enabled people to fly. Longer flights were made when hydrogen gas was used. Hydrogen is lighter than air, but is highly flammable. Great care had to be taken when hydrogen gas was used in balloons. In the mid-1800s, some balloons were made in a long cylinder shape that was tapered at both ends. Engines were later added to power the balloons and push them wherever the pilots wanted them to go.

Curved, Not Flat

3   Scientists and inventors began to experiment with winged aircraft in the late 1800s. Gliders were built. These aircraft did not have any way to power themselves through the air. Once in the air, the pilots were also not able to control the flight. They relied strictly on the lift of air against the wings. Experiments with gliders helped people learn which wing designs worked best. They discovered that curved wings, rather than flat wings, provided the best design for flight. These early flights were important in the achievement of powered airplane flights.

Powered Flight

4   Gliders were not able to stay up in the air for very long. They did not have any way to push themselves through the air. When powered flight was invented in the early 1900s, interest in gliders dropped off.

Changes

5   In the 1920s, people learned more about how to design gliders for longer and more controlled flights. They also learned more about how to keep gliders in the air for longer periods of time even without engines. The body of the glider was made to be as smooth as possible so it could slip more easily through the air. Early gliders were made of wood covered with canvas. Later gliders were made of aluminum. Modern gliders are made of lightweight materials such as fiberglass.

18

The Best Flights

6   Inventors found that long narrow wings produced the best flights. Wings of a glider had to be longer than regular airplanes to help get it into the air and keep it there without an engine. Modern gliders have very sturdy and lightweight wings that provide excellent lifting ability. Some even hold water to give them more weight for faster speeds on long straight flights. The water can be dumped during a flight to make the glider lighter.

Getting Into the Air

7   Without an engine, gliders have several ways of getting into the air. A regular airplane can tow the glider up into the air using a long tow rope attached to the nose of the glider. Once the glider is high enough, its pilot can release the tow rope and soar off. Another way to get a glider into the air uses a powerful engine on the ground. A long cable is attached to the engine at one end of a runway. The other end of the cable is attached to a glider at the opposite end of the runway. The engine winds up the cable, pulling the glider up into the air. The pilot can release the cable at any time.

Hot Air Rises

8   Once a glider is in the air, the pilot tries to keep it aloft as long as possible. Early pilots of gliders usually just flew them straight in for a landing. Pilots then discovered other ways to help keep them in the air. They learned that there are columns of hot air that rise up from the Earth's surface. The sun heats air near the ground. This air expands and goes up. If a glider can find one of these columns, it can go higher by flying in circles to stay with the rising air. The hot air pushes the glider up and up, sometimes thousands of feet.

Mountain High

9   Gliders can ride on wind that blows up as it passes over a mountain. Pilots also look for winds that blow against the side of a mountain or hill before being forced straight up. Either of these wind forces can provide a glider with lift to allow it to stay in the air for a longer period of time.

Which Way to Go?

10   While in flight, the pilot can control the direction the glider flies. Moveable parts on the wings and tail control how the glider, even without an engine, is able to move through the air. Gliders can turn left or right, go up or down, and point to the left or right.

My Notes About What I Am Reading

Just Make It Smooth

11 Landing a glider is much like landing a regular airplane. Gliders usually have only one or two small wheels under the body that let the glider roll smoothly along the runway when it touches down.

12 Most gliders carry only the pilot. Some are able to carry the pilot and one other person. Large gliders are big enough to carry heavy loads into small areas that do not require long landing spaces.

Flying Like a Bird?

13 Gliders are marvelous and beautiful flying machines. Most people who fly in a glider are thrilled. Gliders may be the closest thing people may ever get to being able to fly like a bird.

Timeline of Flight

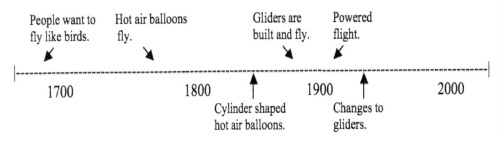

(Category 1 – 2 B – RS)

1. Which word means the same as <u>mimic</u> in paragraph 1?

    A   Change
    B   Check
    C   Control
    D   Copy

(Category 3 – 11 D – RS)

2. Which of the following would be helpful in finding information about landing a glider?

    A   Into the Air
    B   Powered Flight
    C   Which Way to Go?
    D   Just Make It Smooth

20

(Category 3 – 11 A – RS)

3. What is the article mostly about?

    A   Explaining to readers how gliders take off and land
    B   Giving readers information about why gliders were invented
    C   Informing readers about the ways gliders stay in the air
    D   Telling readers about the history of gliders and how they fly

---

(Category 3 – 13 B – SS)

4. What can the reader tell from information provided by the timeline?

    A   Flying gliders is a dangerous activity.
    B   Gliders helped bring about successful powered flight.
    C   People have lost interest in flying like a bird.
    D   Flying gliders is easier than flying balloons.

(Category 3 – 11 B – SS)

5. Which sentence from the selection expresses a fact?

    A   Gliders are marvelous and beautiful flying machines.
    B   Gliders may be the closest thing people may ever get to being able to fly like a bird.
    C   While in flight, the pilot can control the direction the glider flies.
    D   Most people who fly in a glider are thrilled.

THE PUZZLE

Characters – Narrator, Sarah, Mom, Dad

Stage Set – The backdrop shows a back porch on the far left, a front porch with a mailbox on the middle left, a backyard with a bird-house on the middle, a garage full of junk and a bicycle on the middle right, and a living room with boxes of books on the far right

Scene 1

[Sarah and Mom are walking up to their back porch. The stage to the far left shows a back porch door with steps leading up to the door.]

1   **Narrator**: Sarah notices the first envelope as it waves in the breeze blowing gently through the back porch. A piece of clear tape holds it <u>fast</u> to the door frame. The single word "Sarah" is scrawled across the envelope. She has just returned with her mom from a Saturday walking trip to the post office. Sarah is just about ready to finish working on her chores for the day. She has run ahead as they round the corner of their street. The heat of the noon day sun has made both of them thirsty and Sarah is going to fill two tall glasses with ice cold water.

2   **Mom**: *[approaching the back porch]* What is it, Sarah?

3   **Sarah**: *[holding an envelope in both hands]* Someone put this en-velope with my name on it on the door.

4   **Mom**: Well, take a look and see what's inside.

5   **Narrator**: Sarah carefully opens the envelope. She pulls out a jagged piece of paper with unfamiliar markings on it. On the back she finds a message.

6   **Narrator**: Welcome to the Mystery of the Puzzle. Here is your first puzzle piece. There are three more. Find and put all four pieces together and you will have a clue to the location of a great treas-ure. You will find another envelope where the real mail comes.

7   **Sarah**: *[looking up at her mother]* A treasure hunt!

Scene 2

[The stage to the middle left shows the front of a house with a mailbox]

8   **Narrator**: Sarah races around to the front of the house. She is care-ful not to lose the first puzzle piece. Her mom follows close behind.

22

9 **Sarah:** I think it's the mailbox!

10 **Narrator:** Sure enough, Sarah finds another envelope with her name written across the front in red. As her mom pulls up next to her, Sarah tears into the envelope. Out falls a second piece of the puzzle. On the back is another message.

11 Great job! You could try to put these two pieces together but you probably will want to wait until you have the last two pieces. The next one is to be found in the home of your favorite bird.

12 **Sarah:** A mystery, Mom! Someone has started a mystery and I'm going to solve it! [Sarah tucks the puzzle pieces into her shirt pocket.] My favorite bird? That's got to be the Martin birdhouse out back.

13 **Narrator:** Sarah turns and takes off at full speed toward the back yard.

14 **Mom:** I'll catch up to you in a minute. just have to catch my breath.

Scene 3

[The middle of the stage shows a backyard with a birdhouse high on a pole.]

15 **Narrator:** The Martin house is a cluster of birdhouses attached to the top of a tall pole. Every year Sarah and her father repair and repaint these birdhouses. Then the two of them watch as Martins build nests inside and raise their families.

16 Sarah sees the third envelope taped to the pole. She pulls it off and quickly has it opened, seeking the contents inside. The puzzle piece she finds has these words on the back.

17 You're almost there. The last piece of the puzzle is to be found where you keep your bike.

18 **Mom** is just walking up to the Martin house pole. Sarah takes off toward the garage.

19 **Sarah:** The last piece is in the garage!

Scene 4

[The stage to the middle right shows a garage full of junk and a bicycle.]

20 **Narrator:** The garage is a separate building behind the house. The big garage door is kept closed so Sarah enters through a little

My Notes About What I Am Reading

23

door located at the back. Sunlight streams through the single window on the back wall. The inside is covered with dark shadows. Sarah's bicycle is perched against the wall behind some old boxes of clothes next to the cluttered workbench. Taped to the basket on the front of the bicycle is the fourth envelope.

21   Barely able to contain herself, Sarah rips open the envelope. Out falls the last piece of the puzzle. This time there is no message on the back. Sarah removes the other three puzzle pieces and lays all of them down on the dusty garage floor. After several tries, Sarah has the pieces arranged correctly. About this time, her mom arrives in the garage.

22   **Mom**: What does it say, Sarah?

23   **Sarah**: Congratulations! You have solved the mystery of the puzzle. To find your treasure, go to the place where you can go to many places.

24   *[frowning]* A place where you can go to many places. What does that mean? Is it the car, or the TV? Could it be a radio? Mom, where could it be?

25   **Mom**: Sarah, stop and think for a moment. What is it that can take you to many places?

26   **Narrator**: Sarah sits down on her bike and becomes silent, her face all scrunched like she has just sucked on a lemon.

27   **Sarah**: Well, Dad is always telling me that a book can take you to many places. Maybe it's the big bookcase in the living room.

28   **Mom**: Let's go see.

Scene 5

[The stage to the far right shows a living room with boxes.]

29   **Narrator**: They both race across the backyard and into the house. As they trot into the living room, Sarah's dad swivels his chair around and smiles at them.

30   **Dad**: [grinning as he stands up] It took you long enough.

31   **Sarah**: Dad, it was you who wrote me all of those clues and sent me on a treasure hunt?

32   **Dad**: Yes, and here is your treasure.

33   **Narrator**: Sarah looks down. Sprawled across the floor in front of the bookcase are books of all shapes and sizes.

34 **Dad**: Your mom told me how bored you have been getting this summer since school got out. I went down to the library and looked through their collection of used books for sale. I think you will find great treasure in these fine selections. Pick up any one of these books and you will be whisked away to some other place. I know how much you like mysteries so I got you a set of new mystery stories as well. You can repay me by reading all of these books by the end of summer vacation.

35 **Sarah**: Wow! Thanks, Dad! I don't think I will be bored anymore!

36 **Mom**: Well, Sarah, let's get started on these books.

My Notes About What I Am Reading

(Category 1 – 2 E – RS)

1. Read the meanings below for the word <u>fast</u>.

> **fast** (fast) *adjective*
> **1.** quick **2.** firmly attached **3.** ahead of time **4.** loyal

Which meaning best fits the way <u>fast</u> is used in paragraph 1?

A   Meaning 1
B   Meaning 2
C   Meaning 3
D   Meaning 4

2. Read these lines from the play.

> 33 **Narrator:** Sarah looks down. Sprawled across the floor in front of the book-case are books of all shapes and sizes.
>
> 34 **Dad:** Your mom told me how bored you have been getting this summer since school got out. I went down to the library and looked through their collection of used books for sale. I think you will find great treasure in these fine selections. Pick up any one of these books and you will be whisked away to some other place. I know how much you like mysteries so I got you a set of new mystery stories as well. You can repay me by reading all of these books by the end of summer vacation.

What do these lines represent?

A   The reasons Sarah is home for the summer.

B   The ways Sarah keeps busy in the summer.

C   The solution to Sarah's conflict in the story.

D   The way Sarah changes in the story.

(Category 2 – Figure 19 E – SS)

3. Which of these is the best summary of this selection?

A   Someone leaves clues for Sarah all around her house. She wonders who could have left them. Sarah searches and finds her father.

B   Sarah goes to the post office with her mother. She finds envelopes with her name on them. Sarah looks in the garage to find her bicycle.

C   Someone put envelopes with puzzle clues inside for Sarah to find. She looks to see what is in each envelope. Sarah's mother helps her look for the clues.

D   Sarah finds puzzle clues to a mystery. She has to put the pieces together to locate a treasure. Sarah finds her dad and a bunch of books at the end of her hunt.

(Category 2 – 6 A – RS)

4. Why is paragraph 6 important to the selection?

    A   It explains what Sarah is to do to find the treasure.

    B   It tells who made the puzzle pieces for Sarah.

    C   It describes the places Sarah is to go to find the puzzle pieces.

    D   It shows why Sarah is getting a treasure.

(Category 2 – 6 B – RS)

5. How does Sarah feel when she finds the last clue?

    A   Surprised that she finds all of the puzzle pieces

    B   Proud of herself for finding the envelopes all on her own

    C   Disappointed that she is unable to figure out where to look next

    D   Frightened of the dark shadows that are all around in the garage

---

(Category 2 – Figure 19 D – SS)

6. From information found in the passage, what can the reader expect Sarah will do when she gets the treasure?

    A   get ready for school.

    B   sit and read her books.

    C   take her bicycle out for a ride.

    D   help her father clean the garage.

(Category 2 – 5 – SS)

7. How does Scene 5 differ from Scene 1?

    A   Scene 5 contains no dialogue.

    B   Scene 5 takes place in the house.

    C   Scene 5 includes no stage directions.

    D   Scene 5 presents less characters.

Read the selections "Clipper Ships" and "Diary of a Sailor" before answering the questions below.

CLIPPER SHIPS

1   People have traveled on water for thousands of years. Early ships used **oars** to move through the water. Later, simple **sails** were added to harness the wind to power the ships. As time passed and people gained experience with sailing, improvements continued to be made to sailing ships. Voyages grew longer. Ships began to sail <u>abroad</u>. The ships became bigger. They carried cargo back and forth to many parts of the world.

2   Sailing ships were the only way to travel around the world. Ships returned home with many new products and goods. People began to desire these items from other parts of the world. Businesses were set up to bring back goods that people wanted.

3   In the early 1800s, people from the United States had developed a great liking for tea. Faraway China was the only country that was growing a lot of tea at the time. It took sailing ships as long as one year to sail from the United States to China and back again with a load of tea. During the voyage, a lot of the tea spoiled. Faster ships were needed.

4   American ship builders began to make ships that were different than most other sailing ships of the time. Ships were designed that were long and narrow. They did not sit as far down into the water. .More canvas sails were added to the ships. The long, sturdy wooded **masts** that held the sails were made taller. The fronts of these ships were built to move through the water like a knife. Speed was the most important reason designing for these ships.

5   The new ships were given their name because of speed. Someone who walks fast moves "at a fast clip." These ships moved at a fast clip across the oceans so they were called "**clipper** ships".

6   Clipper ships began to sail back and forth to China and other parts of the world in the mid-1800s. They cut the sailing time in half. Now it only took about six months for a ship to

sail from the United States to China and back again. Ships became even faster as people began to learn which routes had the most favorable winds to help speed the ships along.7 Gold was discovered in California in 1848. People wanted to get there as quickly as possible. Clipper ships were used to sail people and goods around South America to the western part of the United States much faster than going over land or sailing on other types of ships would have been. More and more clipper ships were built.

8 Life on clipper ships centered on getting the most speed out of the ships. Ship captains wanted to get their destinations and back home again as quickly as they could. The faster they sailed, the more money they could make for themselves, their crew, and the ships' owners.

9 Many of a clipper ship's crew worked on the sails. The better the sails were set to catch the wind, the faster the ship. The crew had to climb high above the deck of the ship in all kinds of weather to raise or lower the great number of sails. One wrong step and the unlucky sailor could fall from the rigging to the hard deck. Or the sailor might drop into the churning water of the ocean and be left behind.

10 Clipper ships sailed the ocean waters for about twenty-five years. In the 1870s, ships powered by steam engines began to travel the seas. They did not have to rely on wind power to move across the water. No matter how fast the clipper ships could go, if there was no wind these ships were just dead in the water. Steamships could travel with or without wind.

11 Most of the clipper ships had disappeared by the early 1900s. Many were lost at sea or burned. One ship still survives: the **Cutty Sark**. This ship has been restored to look like she did in her early days as a clipper ship. People from all over are able to visit her and imagine what life was like on board this swift ship.

12 The beautiful clipper ships were marvelous, grand sailing vessels to have raced across the open sea.

My Notes About What I Am Reading

DIARY OF A SAILOR

Charles Grant sailed on a sailing ship in the mid-1850s. He kept a diary of his life on the ship as it traveled from San Francisco to China.

April 8, 1852

1   The clipper ship and crew set sail this morning with a strong wind to push us along. The captain expects us to make China in about three months and back again in another three. This is fast. We will be loaded with tea on the return voyage. My watch started at 11:30 a.m. Nothing unusual happened except for a brief rain shower around 3:00 p.m. The wind picked up and I was sent up the rigging to help untangle the ropes holding the main sail. The ropes in the rigging were easy to get free and I was up only about forty feet off the deck. The storm calmed quickly and we set off with full sail once again.

May 8, 1852

2   We have been at sea for about one month. I started to carve a model of our ship out of a beef bone that the cook was about to throw away. I was able to give it three full masts, just like our own ship. I don't have much space here, like any other voyage, but I did find a safe place to keep my carving tools and my sail needle.

May 15, 1852

3   The sea seemed to throw all she had at us today. High winds and huge waves pushed our ship all around. I had to climb way up to the main royal sail, the highest sail on the ship. Climbing past the main sail, the main topsail, and the main top-gallant sail, the rigging was slippery and the winds were fierce. I lost my footing three times. Two times I caught myself with the strength from my own two arms. The third time I would surely have fallen to the deck if it had not been for the quick work of my friend and fellow sailor, Andrew Bridgebain. I had grabbed hold of the yard to pull myself up so I could get my feet on the footropes underneath. There was a sudden gust of wind and the long wooden yard that holds the main royal sail jerked hard to the left. I dug my fingernails into the wood of the yard and hung on. Arthur had climbed the rigging right behind me. He shimmied up the ropes to a spot just under me and steadied my two legs that were dangling off the footropes. I finally managed to get my right foot on the footrope. Arthur put my left foot on the rope. I rested for a few minutes and then we furled the main royal sail. Other sailors were doing the same to all of the other sails. Once this was done, we climbed safely back down to the deck. The ship seemed to settle down. She rode out the storm with only a couple of ropes torn from the rigging. Now

30

we can get back on schedule and get to China and back with the needed tea.

May 16, 1852

4   After the storm passed, the wind stopped completely. Arthur and I spent the better part of our watch helping repair the ropes that had torn away from the rigging. Then we set to work on trying to carve on the main sail of my bone sailing ship. Arthur showed me how to make the sail look like it was full of wind. I can't wait to give this ship to my nephew, Tom, when we sail back into the harbor of San Francisco. I have already carved three ships for me and I know how much Tom is looking forward to this model of my ship. I think I will give the next ship I carve to Arthur.

Glossary

clipper a fast moving ship with tall masts and many sails

Cutty Sark a clipper ship built in England in 1869 that still survives today

mast a tall pole on a ship used to hold sails

oar a long pole with a flat wide blade at one end used to move a boat through the water

sail a piece of fabric that uses the force of wind to move a ship through the water

---

Use "Clipper Ships" to answer questions 1 – 5.

(Category 1 – 2 B – RS)

1. In paragraph 1, the word <u>abroad</u> means

    A   silently.
    B   quickly.
    C   far away.
    D   with great amount.

(Category 3 – 11- C – RS)

2. Clipper ships were built because

    A   people wanted to travel quickly from one place to another.
    B   these ships were easy to make.
    C   these ships used wind to move over the water.
    D   sailors could set the sails.

(Category 3 – 11 A – RS)

3. Paragraph 3 is important to the passage because it

    A   describes a trip to China on a ship.
    B   explains how clipper ships were built.
    C   shows how clipper ships sailed to China.
    D   tells why faster ships were needed.

(Category 3 – 11 D – RS)

4. Where was the Cutty Sark built?

    A   England
    B   United States of America
    C   China
    D   South America

(Category 3 – 14 C – SS)

5. Look at the picture in the passage. What does the reader know about the ship from the picture?

    A   The clipper ship was expensive to repair.

    B   The clipper ship carried much cargo.

    C   The clipper ship had a large crew.

    D   The clipper ship had many sails.

Use "Diary of a Sailor" to answer questions 6 – 8.

(Category 2 – 3 C – SS)

6. How does the author use an important historical event to guide events in this passage?

    A   The author tells why sailors climb up and down ropes on sailing ships to keep the sails open.

    B   The author explains how ship carvings are made out of bone to give as gifts to family members.

    C   The author describes parts of a sailor's trip to China to get tea that is in great demand in the United States.

    D   The author shows that sailors watch out for each other on long sailing voyages.

(Category 2 – Figure 19 D – RS)

7. The reader can tell that Charles

    A   is afraid to climb up the rigging.

    B   has sailed on a ship before.

    C   has trouble making friends.

    D   is older than the other sailors.

(Category 2 – Figure 19 D – RS)

8. Which sentence shows that Arthur was a caring person?

    A   *I think the next ship I carve I will give to Arthur.*

    B   *Arthur had climbed the rigging right behind me.*

    C   *Arthur and I spent the better part of our watch helping repair the ropes that had been torn away from the rigging.*

    D   *The third time I would surely have fallen to the deck if it had not been for the quick work of my friend and fellow sailor, Arthur Bridgebain.*

Use "Clipper Ships" and "Diary of a Sailor" to answer question 9.

(Category 3 – 11 E – RS)

9. One way these selections are alike is that both mention

    A   climbing the rigging to work on the sails.

    B   carving model ships out of beef bones.

    C   ships that were powered by steam engines.

    D   rope in need of repair after a strong storm.

34

Read the next two selections. Then answer the questions that follow them.

THE RELUCTANT SHELTER

1   "It didn't look this hard in the brochure," Miranda muttered as she struggled with the poles of her stiff, recently purchased tent. "Part A is supposed to fit into Part B. But instead, it goes into Part C. This is going to be a long week if this keeps up!"

2   Getting to her feet, Miranda reread the directions and attempted to put the finishing touches on the tent. She hammered the final stake into the ground, careful not to pound so hard as to <u>fracture</u> the piece of wood. She did not need her stakes in many pieces. Miranda stood back to admire her work. The tent promptly fell down.

3   "Oh, no!" Miranda exclaimed. A sudden gust of wind accompanied by large pounding raindrops added to her dismay.

4   "Rain!" sputtered Miranda looking at a thick line of dark clouds rolling in overhead. "No one said anything about rain! The forecast called for partly cloudy skies with slightly cooler temperatures!"

5   Miranda grabbed her backpack and pulled out a pullover sweatshirt jacket with a hood. Quickly, she <u>donned</u> the jacket, relished its warmth, and turned her attention back to the tent.

6   "What went wrong?" she moaned. Miranda reached for the wrinkled sheet of directions that she had carefully placed on the ground with a rock on top to hold it secure next to her back pack. But swirling winds took hold of the single sheet of paper and tossed it just out of her reach. Miranda scrambled after it, slipped in the wet grass, and landed face down in a shallow puddle of muddy water. "I wish I was in better shape."

7   With water dripping off of her face, she pulled herself up in time to see the sheet take off down the hill toward the river. A loud grunt escaped from her lips as she took one last desperate lunge to grab the paper. Her soaked fingers curled around the soggy page.

8   "Ah ha!" shouted Miranda. "Gotch ya!" Clutching the wet directions in her hand, Miranda trudged back to the spot where she had left her crumpled tent. The tent was nowhere in sight. Three other campsites were nearby. Each one had a neat upright tent protecting its inhabitants from the driving rain. But not one of them boasted an extra tent.

9   "Where's my tent?" whined an exasperated Miranda. "It may not have been up, but at least it was here."

10 Frantically, Miranda searched the surrounding area. The rain stopped and the wind died down. Finally, she found her tent wrapped around a thin sapling on the other side of a small hill. The tree was the last obstacle on the tent's path toward the river. Without that sapling to stop it, Miranda decided, the tent would be well on its way downriver.

11 With a sigh of relief, Miranda untangled the tent from the tree, carried it back to her camp ground, smoothed out the directions, and methodically attempted to again put up her tent.

12 Three of Miranda's fellow campers wandered by during her struggles. One even offered to help after mentioning that she had watched Miranda earlier chase after the sheet of directions. Miranda thanked them all, but politely declined and patiently continued on her own. She wanted to be able to provide for and take care of herself.

13 After 60 grueling minutes during which the tent collapsed two more times, Miranda was able to erect her tent. Exhausted, she pulled her backpack inside, rummaged through her clothes, and produced one dry shirt with two pairs of pants. The other garments would need sitting out in a full day of sun to dry. Her waterproof sleeping bag proved its worth as Miranda snuggled in for a short nap before supper.

14 "I hope supper isn't going to be this difficult," Miranda mumbled drifting off to sleep.

UP

1   Tina looked around at her new tent. All seemed to be in order. She thought of the time it took her to erect the tent and remembered how effortless it seemed. She did not even have to read the directions. The tent poles snapped right into place. Each tent stake hammered smoothly into the ground. All of the ropes pulled tight, straining evenly to keep the tall corners upright. Everything was so taut Tina could bounce a quarter off any square inch of fabric on her tent. The floor laid out smooth, unspoiled by any lumps on the soft bed of grass under the tent. The wind had even cooperated, withering to a mere whisper as Tina put up her shelter with ease.

36

2   Now, the wind had picked up considerably. Thick, billowing clouds began to move in overhead. Climbing out of her tent, Tina looked up just in time to see a girl chase after a piece of paper. The paper was a rocket on its way toward the river. Tina began to follow the girl and offer to help, but she was interrupted by another camper.

3   "Tina, the camp counselor needs you at the main cabin right away. Your mom is on the phone," said Marcella.

4   Worried that something was wrong, Tina rushed to the main cabin.

5   "Mom, what's the matter" asked a breathless Tina.

6   "Everything is fine here, Tina," answered her mother. "How are you doing? We had some rough weather around here and saw that it was headed in your direction. Your father and I wanted to make sure that you were okay."

7   "I am fine," Tina replied. "Some dark clouds are beginning to roll through and rain is beginning to fall, but it is not bad. Remember I came here to show that I can do things on my own and be okay."

8   "That is great, dear. Your father says hello. We will let you get back to camping. See you in a week," said Tina's mother.

9   "Bye mom," Tina answered. She hung up the phone and walked back to her tent. It was raining pretty hard now. Tina looked for but did not find the girl who had been chasing the paper.

10 Climbing into her dry tent, she took one last glance around and said, "What happened to her?"

11 With <u>ample</u> time before supper, Tina pulled out her clothes and tried to focus her attention on arranging them into daily attire for the week. She couldn't stop thinking about that girl. After trying to match a pair of polka dot green pants with a striped blouse, Tina decided to give up and look again. Opening the flap of her tent, she peeked out. She saw that the girl had returned and was trying to put up her tent. Tina walked over to the girl.

12 "Hi! My name is Tina. Do you need any help putting up your tent?" asked Tina. "I noticed that you were running after a piece of paper earlier. I thought it might be the directions."

13 "Yes, it was," replied the other girl. "My name is Miranda. Thank you so much for offering to help me, but I want to finish putting up my tent by myself. The competition to see who can set up a tent the quickest is first thing tomorrow and I want to be ready."

37

14 "Sure, I understand," Tina said. "Maybe we can get together for supper. I hear we are going to have pigs in a blanket."

15 "That would be great," said Miranda. "Thanks."

16 Tina walked back to her tent.

17 Crawling back inside, Tina whispered to herself, "Now let's see what I can find to match with these polka dot pants."

My Notes About What I Am Reading

Use "The Reluctant Shelter" to answer questions 1 – 4.

(Category 1 – 2 B – RS)

1. In paragraph 5, the author uses the word <u>donned</u> to indicate that Miranda

    A found a jacket.

    B switched a jacket.

    C put on a jacket.

    D moved over a jacket.

(Category 2 – 6 A – RS)

2. How do paragraphs 11 through 13 show that Miranda solves her main problem in the passage?

    A Miranda is able to dry out her clothes.

    B Miranda is able to prepare supper.

    C Miranda is able to talk to her mother on a phone.

    D Miranda is able to put up her tent.

(Category 2 – Figure 19 D – RS)

3. Which sentence from the passage supports the idea that this is the first time Miranda has put up a tent?

    A   *Miranda stood back to admire her work.*

    B   *After 60 grueling minutes during which the tent collapsed two more times, Miranda was able to erect her tent.*

    C   *"It didn't look this hard in the brochure," Miranda muttered as she struggled with the poles of her stiff, recently purchased tent.*

    D   *Miranda reached for the crumpled sheet of directions she had carefully placed on the ground with a rock on top to hold it secure next to her backpack.*

(Category 1 – 2 E – RS)

4. Read the definitions of the word <u>fracture</u>.

    > **fracture** (frak' chər) *noun*   **1.** a break   **2.** the appearance of the surface of a mineral
    >
    > *verb*   **1.** to cause a break   **2.** to go beyond the limits of rules

    Which definition best shows how <u>fracture</u> is used in paragraph 2 of the story?

    A   Definition 1 - noun

    B   Definition 2 - noun

    C   Definition 1 - verb

    D   Definition 2 - verb

Use "Up" to answer questions 5 – 8.

(Category 1 – 2 B – RS)

5. What does the word <u>ample</u> mean in paragraph 11?

    A   Busy
    B   Enough
    C   Quiet
    D   Unexpected

(Category 2 – 6 A – RS)

6. What happens when Tina starts to follow Miranda?

    A   Tina gets a telephone call from her mother.
    B   Tina offers to help Miranda look for the directions.
    C   Tina tries to get her clothes ready for the week.
    D   Tina wonders what to do before supper.

(Category 2 – 8 A – RS)

7. Read this sentence from the passage.

    > **The paper was a rocket on its way toward the river.**

    The author uses these words to

    A   show the speed of the wind.
    B   describe the shape of the paper.
    C   explain the location of the river.
    D   tell the force of the water.

8. Read the first sentence of a summary of the passage.

Summary of "Up"

Tina remembers how she put her tent together. _____
_____

Which set of sentences best completes the summary?

A   Tina tries to follow a girl who is running after a piece of paper. She loses the girl and goes to sort her clothes. Tina waits for supper to arrive.

B   Tina talks to her mom on the phone, who tells her a bad storm is on its way to the camp. Tina says everything is okay.

C   Tina notices how nice her tent looks. A storm is coming. Tina gets in her tent to keep from getting wet.

D   Tina sees a girl chasing a piece of paper. Tina gets a phone call from her mom, who is checking on her. Tina offers to help the girl put up her tent.

Use "The Reluctant Shelter" and "Up" to answer question 9.

(Category 1 – 3 A – SS)

9. Which sentence best represents the theme found in both passages?

A   Getting in shape is good.

B   Living in nature is fun.

C   Caring for oneself is important.

D   Putting up a tent takes a lot of skill.

| | My Notes About What I Am Reading |

FREDERICK DOUGLASS

1   Frederick Douglass was born as Frederick Bailey sometime around 1818. He was born a slave in the state of Maryland. He lived his early life with his grandmother. Frederick's mother died when he was about seven years old.

2   When Frederick was eight years old, he was moved to Baltimore, Maryland, to work as a slave. His owner's wife began to teach Frederick how to read. She had to stop. Her husband told her it was against the law to teach a slave how to read. He said that if slaves could read and write, they might start to think about freedom. Frederick continued to learn on his own. With the help of other people, he did learn to read and write. Frederick learned about other slaves escaping to be free or buying their own freedom. He too wanted to be free like the wind.

3   Frederick was moved around and worked for other people. In 1835, he planned to escape. The plan was discovered and Frederick was put in jail. Then he was sent back to Baltimore. There Frederick was put to work in the shipyards.

4   While in Baltimore, Frederick met free African Americans. One was Anna Murray. She helped him escape to New York in 1838. He changed his last name to Douglass and married Anna Murray. They moved to Massachusetts.

5   Frederick worked hard to support his family. He worked in the shipyard, shoveled coal, and cleaned out chimneys. In 1841, Frederick began to work for a newspaper that spoke out against slavery. He began to go to other cities and give talks about how slavery was wrong. Frederick told about how children were separated from their parents and husbands from their wives. He spoke about whippings that were <u>inflicted</u> on slaves. Frederick talked about the harsh conditions slaves lived under.

6   In 1845, Frederick wrote a book about his life, The Narrative of the Life of Frederick Douglass, An American Slave. He traveled to England to tell people about slavery. Friends of his in England bought his freedom in 1846. He could now go home a free person. Frederick returned to the United States in 1847. He moved to the state of New York and started his own newspaper. He wrote about the injustices of slavery. He told of the unfavorable ways African Americans were treated.

7 The Civil War was fought in the United States from 1861 to 1865. Southern states wanted to maintain slavery, while northern states wanted to end slavery. The two sides fought for many long years. African American soldiers helped fight in the northern army.

8 The southern army was defeated in 1865. Slavery was abolished a few months after the war with the passage of the Thirteenth Amendment to the United States Constitution. Whiles slaves had now become free, many problems still existed for African Americans. They were treated unfairly and unjustly. Many lived in poverty. Laws were passed in many southern states to prevent African Americans from being able to vote and to segregate them. African Americans were not allowed to mingle with other people. Improvements in the rights of African Americans would come slowly.

9 Frederick Douglass wrote two other books about his life. One was My Bondage and My Freedom. The other was The Life and Times of Frederick Douglass.

10 The last years of his life saw Frederick speaking out about harsh treatment of African Americans in the south. Frederick Douglass died in 1895.

My Notes About What I Am Reading

(Category 1 – 2 A – RS)

1. In paragraph 5, the word <u>inflicted</u> means

    A arranged.

    B caused.

    C found.

    D set.

(Category 2 – 6 A – RS)

2. What happened after Frederick Douglass wrote the book The Narrative of the Life of Frederick Douglass, An American Slave?

    A Douglass escaped to New York.

    B Douglass married Anna Murray.

    C Douglass joined the northern army to fight in the Civil War of the United States.

    D Douglass started his own newspaper.

43

3. Which of these is the best summary of this passage?

    A   Born as a slave, Frederick Douglass lived in the southern United States. He escaped to freedom and went to England. Frederick Douglass wrote several books about his life.

    B   Frederick Douglass was a slave in the southern part of the United States. When he was 20 years old he was able to get his freedom. Married and with children, he worked hard to provide for his family.

    C   Born in the early 1800s, Frederick Douglass worked as a slave for many owners. He dreamed of freedom. In 1838, he escaped from slavery and moved to Massachusetts. He was married and had several children.

    D   Frederick Douglass lived his early life as a slave. After gaining his freedom, he helped tell others about the lives of slaves. After slavery ended, he talked to people about how African Americans were treated in the southern United States.

(Category 2 – Figure 19 D – SS)

4. Which sentence from the passage shows that slaves had a difficult life?

    A   *Frederick worked hard to support his family.*

    B   *His owner's wife began to teach Frederick how to read.*

    C   *African-American soldiers helped fight in the northern army.*

    D   *Frederick told how children were separated from their parents and husbands from their wives.*

(Category 2 – Figure 19 D – SS)

5. From information found in the passage presented by the author, the reader can conclude that

    A   it took a long time for the effects of slavery to disappear.

    B   slavery was important to the country of England.

    C   newspapers treated slaves with respect and dignity.

    D   the end of the Civil War made life easy for newly freed slaves.

(Category 2 – 7 A – SS)

6. Read this sentence from the passage.

> **He too wanted to be free like the wind.**

The author uses these words to

    A   show the reader how Frederick worked to find a job.

    B   describe Frederick's journey to escape from slavery.

    C   explain Frederick's desire to be able to live on his own.

    D   tell the reader what Frederick did to support his family.

Read the selection "I Made It on My Own" before answering the questions below.

I MADE IT ON MY OWN

1   My life did not start so well. I, Sarah Breedlove, was born in 1867 to former slaves. My parents were sharecroppers. They rented farm land. Most of what they grew went to the land owner. They were having a difficult time getting ahead.

2   I have an older brother and sister. When I was seven years old, my parents died of yellow fever. My brother, sister, and I tried to stay together and continue to work the land, but our crops did not do very well. My sister and I moved to Mississippi when I was ten. We washed other people's clothes for our living. In 1882, I married Moses McWilliams and had a daughter, Lelia, in 1885. My husband died two years later.

3   In 1888, I moved with my daughter to St. Louis, Missouri. I started and ran a laundry business. I did many things to improve my life. Lelia did well in school and went to college in Tennessee. It was during this time in St. Louis that I began to have problems with my hair.

4   My hair is very thin and some of it is beginning to come out. I think my hair is not pretty. I have tried products to help my hair grow back and get thicker. Nothing seems to work. I have decided to make my own hair grower. My hair is now growing in thicker than before. The hair-grower works on my friends, too. I have the idea to sell her invention to other women.

5   At this time, there are few products on the market that African-American women can use on their problem hair. I am <u>frank</u> and open about women's hair and scalp problems. I tell women of my problems and how I can help them. I am able to sell my product quite well. I go door-to-door to sell. I hire other women to sell my hair product.

6   I have developed and made other hair care products besides one to grow hair. Shampoo and hair sheen have also been invented as well as other products to help the hair look nice.

7   I have lived in Denver, Colorado. In 1906, I married Charles Joseph Walker. I changed my name to Madam C. J. Walker. This is the name that I have put on my hair products. My business has grown and grown. A beauty college was started in Pennsylvania in 1908. My daughter, Lelia, freshly graduated from college, helped me run the college and train women to care for hair.

46

8   In 1910, I moved the company to Indiana. A factory has been built there to make all of my hair care products. More and more people have begun to work for the company. I have opened beauty shops in many cities in the United States and South America. My businesses were a gold mine.

9   I used the money I made from my hair products to help many people besides my family. I aided the people who worked for me as well as many schools, churches, hospitals, children's homes, and other needy people. I tried to help other women and African Americans start businesses of their own. I knew that this would create more jobs for people. I have spoken about this all over the United States.

10 I am quite wealthy. I am the first African American woman to have earned my own money to become a millionaire. I have been a role model to many other people who wanted to make a better life for themselves.

My Notes About What I Am Reading

(Category 2 – 7 A – SS)

1. What can the reader tell about Madam C. J. Walker's beliefs from this passage?

    A   She thought it was necessary to have a lot of money.
    B   She thought money was important to help people be happy.
    C   She thought it was necessary to start businesses everywhere she lived.
    D   She thought it was important for people to be able to make their own lives better.

(Category 1 – 2 B – RS)

2. What does the word <u>frank</u> mean in paragraph 5?

    A   Calm
    B   Confusing
    C   Encouraging
    D   Honest

(Category 2 – Figure 19 D – SS)

3. From information found in the passage, the reader can tell that

    A   Sarah Breedlove felt it was important to help other people.

    B   Sarah Breedlove liked to move to new places.

    C   Many people died of yellow fever.

    D   Pennsylvania has many beauty colleges.

(Category 2 – 6 A – RS)

4. Paragraph 3 is important to the passage because it

    A   describes why Sarah moved around when she was a young girl.

    B   shows what Sarah's parents did for a living.

    C   tells about Sarah's difficulty with her hair.

    D   explains how Sarah invented hair care products.

(Category 2 – Figure 19 E – SS)

5. Look at the information in the outline.

    > I. Sarah Breedlove's early life with her parents
    >   A.   Born to former slave parents
    >   B.   Day-to-day living was hard
    >   C.   _____
    >   D.   Most of her family's crop went to the land owner

    Which idea would best fit in the blank?

    A   Lived on rented land

    B   Moved to Mississippi

    C   Washed other people's clothes

    D   Opened a factory in Indiana

6. Read this sentence from the passage.

> **My businesses were a gold mine.**

The author uses this sentence to

A   tell where Madam Walker put her businesses.

B   describe the success of Madam Walker's businesses.

C   show the age of Madam Walker's businesses.

D   explain why Madam Walker started her businesses.

49

Read the selections "The Erie Canal" and "Nathan's Journey" before answering the questions below.

THE ERIE CANAL

1   "Low bridge! Everybody down!" shouted the captain as the boat approached the bridge across the canal. This warning was a common sound on the many boats and barges that crossed back and forth on the Erie Canal in the mid-1800s.

2   Before the days of roads and trains, water routes were the best way to move people and goods across the country. But these also presented problems. Rivers and streams could overflow or dry up. Some parts of rivers or streams were too shallow. Many rivers also contained waterfalls and fast rough water called "rapids". Many water routes did not link up easily to each other or they just did not go where people wanted them to go. "Canals", or man-made waterways, were the answer.

3   Canals have been around for thousands of years. Early China constructed a vast system of canals to get from place to place and to move goods. The Roman Empire used canals to transport its armies. Countries in Europe also built these man-made waterways.

4   After the Revolutionary War, the United States was eager to explore and expand its boundaries. People dreamed of a way to join the eastern part of the country with the Great Lakes in the middle part of North America. People and goods would then be able to travel from the Atlantic Ocean all the way to Lake Erie and back again. This would allow goods to be traded back and forth between Europe, Asia, the United States, and other countries of the world.

5   Work on the Erie Canal began on July 4, 1817. When completed, the canal was to be 363 miles long connecting Buffalo, New York in the west with the Hudson River in the east. The Hudson River flowed past New York City to the Atlantic Ocean. Thousands of workers helped to build the canal. It took over eight years to complete the work.  A four-feet-deep and forty-foot-wide trench was dug out of the earth. Trees had to be cut down and their stumps removed, and

thick groups of plants growing along the ground had to be cleared away. Explosives were used to remove large amounts of rock. Bridges had to be built across the canal so local people could cross over.

6   In some places along the canal, the level of the land changed quickly. Locks had to be built to raise or lower boats so they could move smoothly along the length of the canal. A boat floated into a lock and was closed in by watertight gates at either end. Water was drained from the lock if the boat needed to be lowered. Water was allowed into the lock from the higher level if the boat needed to be raised. Once the proper level was achieved, the lock gate opened and the boat was free to move on.

7   The Erie Canal crossed many rivers along its path. Stone bridges called "aqueducts" were built to carry the canal across these spots. Then, traffic along the route was able to move smoothly and was uninterrupted.

8   Horses and mules were used to pull boats along the smooth water of the canal. Mules were used more often. They were <u>hardy</u> animals that could work for long periods of time. A long rope connected the horses or mules with the boat. A young boy of maybe ten or eleven years old walked the animals on a path built right along the side of the canal.

9   The governor of New York, DeWitt Clinton, was a strong supporter of the Erie Canal. Even before he was elected governor, he worked hard to bring the canal into existence. When the canal project had difficulty obtaining money to finish the route, the New York legislature provided the needed funds. Finally, in October of 1825, the Erie Canal was officially completed. Governor Clinton was on hand as well as hundreds of other people for the celebration.

10   The Erie Canal cut the travel time between New York City and Buffalo, New York, from several weeks to eight days. People and goods could go back and forth for less money. Buffalo soon became a busy trading center. Thousands of settlers also came to Buffalo to go off and settle the lands of Ohio, Indiana, and other places in the middle of North America.

11   The Erie Canal carried people and cargo for many years. Over time, it was made larger and other improvements were made, such as electric locks and the use of tugboats to pull barges along the canal. It was closed to transporting goods in 1994. The Erie Canal is now used mostly by people for swimming or boating.

My Notes About What I Am Reading

51

NATHAN'S JOURNEY

1   Nathan looked out across the canal to the team of mules that pulled the boat through the water. Each step of the team brought his family that much closer to Buffalo. From there, he and his family would travel on to Ohio. They hoped to start a new life on a large farm. He was quite excited.

2   A low bridge showed itself up ahead. Nathan saw the captain of the boat prepare himself for the warning. Then it came.

3   "Low bridge! Everybody down!" shouted the captain. People all over the boat ducked their heads and waited for the slow moving boat to cross under the bridge. Once passed, the people straightened up and went on about their business.

4   Nathan's family had waited several years for this opportunity. Up until now his father had wanted to wait for the new canal to open. He had said it would make the journey to Ohio much easier. The family was also able to save more money to help with the move.

5   After the Erie Canal had opened in 1825, Nathan's father had readied the family for a late summer move from New York to Ohio. Now they were almost to the western end of the canal. In a few days they would land in Buffalo and make their way to a new home. Nathan knew it would be a lot of work but he figured his family would be better off and have a good chance to improve their lives.

6   "Come sit with us, Nathan," said his mother. "It is time for lunch and you need to eat so you will be strong and fit for the new farm."

Use "Erie Canal" to answer questions 1 – 8.

(Category 3 – 11 C – RS)

1.   People wanted to build a canal across the state of New York to

    A   move supplies to the army.

    B   make Buffalo a major trading city.

    C   allow goods to be shipped back and forth.

    D   help provide jobs for people.

52

(Category 3 – 11 C – RS)

2. How were the canals built by the Roman Empire different than the Erie Canal?

   A   The canals built by the Roman Empire carried soldiers.

   B   The canals built by the Roman Empire were used for swimming.

   C   The canals built by the Roman Empire were used for fishing.

   D   The canals built by the Roman Empire carried rocks.

(Category 3 – Figure 19 D – RS)

3. The reader can tell that mules

   A   are strong.

   B   are lazy.

   C   cannot walk fast.

   D   cannot work long hours.

(Category 1 – 2 B – RS)

4. In paragraph 8, the word <u>hardy</u> means

   A   calm.

   B   patient.

   C   steady.

   D   tough.

5. Which of these is the best summary of the passage?

    A   The Erie Canal was built in the early 1800s. It helped people get from the east to the west. The governor of New York helped get it built.

    B   The Erie Canal was built to carry people and goods across New York. It took many years and lots of work to complete. The canal helped open up the west to trade and new settlements.

    C   People wanted to travel from east to the west across North America. The Erie Canal was built. It had many low bridges so people could cross over from one side to the other.

    D   People dreamed of trading with people from other lands. The Erie Canal was built so goods could be traded with other countries. The canal crossed a lot of rivers.

(Category 3 – Figure 19 D – RS)

6. Which sentence from the passage shows that the canal ran into problems during its construction?

    A   *Bridges had to be built across the canal so local people could cross over.*

    B   *Locks had to be built to raise or lower boats so they could move smoothly along the length of the canal.*

    C   *When completed, the canal was to be 363 miles long connecting Buffalo, New York in the west with the Hudson River in the east.*

    D   *When the canal project had difficulty obtaining money to finish the route, the legislature of New York provided the needed funds.*

(Category 3 – 10 A – SS)

7. The author most likely wrote this passage to

    A tell readers of the jobs made by people who developed land.
    B show to readers the reasons that people moved west.
    C explain to readers how a new route to the western part of the United States came to be.
    D describe to readers what people did to start new lives in different parts of the United States.

(Category 3 – 11 D – RS)

8. From information provided by the map, the reader can tell that another canal moved through which state to help people move westward?

    A Ohio
    B Pennsylvania
    C New Jersey
    D Virginia

Use "Nathan's Journey" to answer question 9.

(Category 2 – 3 C – SS)

9. How does the author use an historical event to guide events in this passage?

    A The author tells of a family's trip to start a new life.
    B The author explains that mules were used to move cargo.
    C The author describes what people did to stay strong.
    D The author shows how people saved money for their future.

| **My Notes About What I Am Reading** |

FLAMINGOS

1   A faint noise rings across the shallow water. A long bright orange neck stretches high while the head on top turns from side to side. Two yellow eyes search all around. Other necks reach up and heads turn. They are looking, too. Nothing is found. All heads return to the water. The flamingos continue feeding in the small lake filled with salt water. This is their home.

2   These colorful birds have been around for thousands of years. In the wild, many live on the islands and along the coasts of the Caribbean. Other flamingos live in southern Europe, Asia, and Africa.

3   The flamingo is the tallest wading bird and one of the most brilliantly colored. Adult flamingos can range in color from a bright pink to orange to a deep red. They get their color from the food that they eat. Most wild flamingos live near salt water. The tiny plants and animals that flamingos eat live in this water. The food contains the same kind of chemicals that turn carrots orange. The flamingos consume these chemicals in their food and turn different shades of orange or red. Baby flamingos usually have white feathers. They have not yet developed the beautiful, colorful feathers of their elders.

4   The top bill of a flamingo is hinged and is able to move up and down like the lower jaw on a person. Flamingos eat with their heads upside down. They twist their necks around and stick their heads under the water. Their bills are curved to help catch food more easily. The top bill opens and closes allowing the birds to quickly search for food. The edges of the black upper and lower bills are lined with tiny teeth like those of a comb. The flamingos use their tongues to push out the water through the teeth, trapping food inside their mouths.

5   Flamingos spend a large part of their day looking for food and eating. Long slender legs allow the tall birds to walk through the shallow water of a lake or pond in search of food. Items on their menu include tiny insects, brine shrimp, seeds, and algae. The food is so small it takes a lot to satisfy the flamingos' hunger.

56

6   Being social animals, flamingos like to be around other flamingos. They make honking noises as they move around each other through the water looking for food. Flamingos feed together and rest together, too. One way that they rest is to lift one leg out of the water and fold it underneath their bodies. They balance on their other stiff leg while resting their heads on their backs.

7   Beautiful, colorful feathers protect the flamingos and keep them warm and dry. When not eating or resting, flamingos are cleaning, or "preening", their feathers. They use their bills to pull out old feathers and make sure that the others are neat and clean. This constant chore helps keep their feathers waterproof.

8   Flamingos live in or near very salty water. Their bodies have a special part that removes the salt from the water after they drink it. This enables the birds to survive without fresh water.

9   Adult flamingos are able to fly. They stretch their long wings and black feathers appear. These flight feathers provide the lift the birds need to fly. Once in the air, the graceful birds extend their long necks out in front and their thin legs behind. Flying at speeds up to thirty miles per hour, flamingos move around, usually searching for food.

10 A single baby chick is born to flamingo parents each nesting season. A nest made of mud is built by the parents in the shape of a cone. After hatching from an egg, the weak, short-legged chick stays under the care of its parents. Young flamingos are unable to fend for themselves. The parents feed their chick a special liquid called "crop milk". Made in the throat of the parent, this food gives the chick the nutrition it needs to grow. Flamingo chicks eat this way until their own bills turn dark and curve downward so they can eat upside down like adult flamingos.

11 Flamingos have few natural enemies. People can do the greatest harm to them. Land that serves as the feeding and nesting grounds of flamingos is slowly being taken over by people, roads, homes, and recreational uses. The flamingo is being forced to move elsewhere. Places that are appropriate for flamingos to live are becoming scarcer. To help, flamingos are protected by laws and special places have been set aside that prevent people from entering the flamingos' habitat.

12 Flamingos are one of the most interesting animals to observe and study. Most people will never see a flamingo in the wild, but zoos and animal parks give people chances to learn more about them. These beautifully feathered creatures provide a wonderful insight into the world of nature.

SUNSET BIRD

by Sally Lyons

1   Bent black beak at the
Tip of an S,
Salmon-colored softness
To a great plumed feathered crest.

5   Knees that pop backwards
Bending at an angle,
So many spiny spindles
Make a great tangle.

9   Graceful head lowering
Disappearing underneath,
Grabbing little shrimp
Sure to be a totally tasty treat,
Mmm, Mmm, Mmm.

14   Resting on one leg
With the other tucked away,
Eyes barely shut
At the closing of the day.

18   The ballet of the feathered creature,
Beautiful and slow,
The dancing bobbing movements
Of the pink flamingo.

Use "Flamingos" to answer questions 1 - 4.

(Category 3 – 11 C – RS)

1. Why do flamingos spend most of their time looking for food?

    A   Their food is so small it takes them a while to get their fill.
    B   Their food is hard to find and it takes them a while to find it.
    C   Flamingos eat upside down and it is hard to get food that way.
    D   Flamingos like to be around other flamingos as they eat.

(Category 1 – 2 E – RS)

2. Read the meanings below for the word <u>season</u>.

---

season (sē' zən) *noun*   **1.** any of the times of the year: winter, spring, summer, or fall   **2.** the time when something takes place

season (sē' zən) *verb*   **1.** to make food more tasty   **2.** to make more usable

---

Which meaning best fits the way <u>season</u> is used in paragraph 10?

A   Any of the times of the year: winter, spring, summer, or fall

B   The time when something takes place

C   To make food more tasty

D   To make more usable

(Category 3 – 11 A – RS)

3. Look at this chart of information.

Unable to fly	Eat crop milk
Flamingo Chicks	
Unable to feed themselves	

Which detail belongs in the empty box?

A   Long legs

B   Curved beaks

C   White feathers

D   Black bills

59

(Category 3 – 11 D – RS)

4. The author most likely uses the picture of the flamingo to help the reader

    A   know what the flamingo eats.
    B   see the shape of the flamingo's neck.
    C   see the size of the flamingo's feathers.
    D   know how the flamingo flies.

Use "Sunset Bird" to answer questions 5 - 7.

(Category 2 – 4 A – SS)

5. The author uses the words "Mmm, Mmm, Mmm" to

    A   show the reader how flamingo feels about the food.
    B   tell the reader what the flamingo does to find another flamingo.
    C   describe to the reader why a flamingo stands on one leg.
    D   explain to the reader who a flamingo likes to visit.

(Category 2 – 8 A – RS)

6. What was the author's purpose in using the phrase "at the tip of an S"?

    A   To tell how a flamingo rests
    B   To explain how a flamingo sounds
    C   To describe the shape of a flamingo
    D   To show what a flamingo does to stand

(Category 2 – 4 A – SS)

7. Read this line from the poem.

> **Sure to be a totally tasty treat,**

The author uses these words to

A   help the reader understand what a flamingo does to move.

B   help the reader understand why a flamingo closes its eyes.

C   let the reader know that the shrimp satisfies the flamingo.

D   let the reader know that the sunset affects how a flamingo eats.

Use "Flamingos" and "Sunset Bird" to answer questions 8 - 9.

(Category 3 – 11 E – RS)

8. Both the poem and the article mention the head and bill of the flamingo to

A   explain how flamingos get food.

B   tell of the flamingos' beauty.

C   show where the flamingos' homes are found.

D   describe how the flamingos move around.

(Category 1 – Figure 19 F – RS)

9. An idea presented in both passages is the

A   protection provided by feathers.

B   care parent flamingos give to their young.

C   long searching for daily meals.

D   How colorful flamingos are.

CHARROS

1   The young charros, or cowboys, enter the arena sitting atop their prancing horses. Eager for the competition to begin, David searches the stands for his family. Finally, he spots them a few rows from the railing surrounding the arena. He removes his sombrero and waves it over his head at them. David's family returns the greeting with their own sombrero waving.

2   The events of the day begin. Each charro takes a turn galloping back into the arena. Near the center, each rider pulls back on the reins and the horse skids to a stop. Then each rider spins his horse to the right and to the left. Next the rider directs his horse to walk backwards. This event ends with each charro greeting the judges of the competition.

3   David is the fourth rider into the arena. He gallops in on his horse and they both perform without a hitch. David is excited. He wants to do well. This is his first charreada, or riding <u>competition</u>.

4   David works hard and does his best at each event. He lassos horses, pulls a young bull down by its tail, and rides a small bull. Now it is time for his favorite event. David and two of his best friends ready themselves for the calf roping competition.

5   Sitting motionless in their saddles, the three friends wait for the release of the young calf. Suddenly the calf bolts out of the gate. David and his two companions, Ricky and Gerrado, follow. Ricky twirls his rope over his head and focuses on the calf's head. Gerrado lags a bit behind to lasso the hind legs of the calf. Teams of riders have to work together to successfully complete the event safely.

6   Ricky and Gerrado lasso the calf at the same time. They pull the legs out from under the calf and it falls to the ground. David quickly gets off of his horse and unties the calf. Howling at the top of its lungs but unhurt, the young calf trots off and leaves the arena through the exit gate. David looks over at the other two boys and grins. He knows that he has done his best. Now they must get ready for the next event.

7   Throughout Mexico young charros train for the charreada. They learn the history and traditions of Mexico's charros. Practicing skills handed down from older family members, they learn to ride horses and calves, spin lariats, and rope horses and calves. They also learn the values of their ancestors, which are carefully handed down

from generation to generation. Pride, honesty, and honor are instilled in each young charro. Each time a charreada is held, these traditions will be remembered and celebrated.

SECOND BEST

1　Juan crouches low in the saddle. His excitement mounts. He has worked long and hard for this moment. Grabbing the worn leather reins in his left hand and the stiff curled rope in his right hand, he readies himself for the starter's horn. Juan's eyes are fixed on the wooden gate blocking his path. He lets out a deep sigh. Like other charreadas before, waiting is never easy for him. Juan knows that he has prepared well, but one never knows what will happen. The history of the charros and charreadas has proven its value in providing fine young riders. Juan is no exception.

2　"BLEEP!" the horn sounds above and behind him. Junior, Juan's loyal brown and white pinto horse, lurches forward as the gate swings open before them. A black and white blur speeds past on the right. Knees bent and his hand held high over his head, Juan spins his rope in a tight circle. Junior <u>tears</u> after the calf, gaining on it with each gallop.

3　Suddenly, the calf veers off to the side. Like syrup on a pancake, Junior stays right on the bawling calf. Juan twirls the rope two more revolutions and lets it fly toward the calf. Arching through the air, the open loop of the rope falls cleanly over the swaying head of the calf. Juan quickly jerks back on the rope while at the same time wrapping it around the horn on his saddle. Junior immediately stops short, pulling the rope taut. The calf is knocked down, all of its legs flailing in the air. Juan jumps off Junior and races to the calf. Before it can rise, Juan grabs the calf's two hind legs and pulls out a short length of rope. With great speed, he wraps the rope around the two legs. Then he grasps one of the calf's front legs and winds the remainder of the rope around it. Done, he throws his hands into the air signaling his completion of the task.

4　"Thirteen point five seconds!" blares a voice over a loud speaker. "Second best time today!" The crowd whoops and hollers.

5　"Way to go, Charro Juan!" yells someone in the crowd.

6　"Great charreada!" shouts another.

7　Juan reaches down and carefully unwraps the rope from around the legs of the calf. Then he gently removes the loop from around

63

its neck. Still bawling but unhurt, the calf scrambles to his feet and trots off in search of its mother. Juan coils his rope and ties it onto the side of his saddle. Junior stands still all the while.

8   Placing his left boot in the stirrup, Juan grabs onto the saddle horn, swings his other leg over Junior's back, and hoists himself into the saddle that has been in his family since his grandfather was a boy. Grabbing the reins with both hands, Juan guides Junior across the dusty arena toward the exit gate. The people packed into the wooden benches surrounding the arena clap their approval. The crowd knows Juan will be back for next year's competition in his favorite event to try and best the other ropers.

Use "Second Best" to answer questions 1 - 3.

(Category 1 – 2 E – RS)

1.   Read the meanings below for the word <u>tears</u>.

> **tears** (terz) *verb* **1.** disturbs **2.** pulls apart **3.** moves with great speed **4.** divides with doubt

Which meaning best fits the way <u>tears</u> is used in paragraph 2?

A   Meaning 1
B   Meaning 2
C   Meaning 3
D   Meaning 4

(Category 2 – Figure 19 D – RS)

2.   The reader can tell from the story that Juan will

A   try another event.
B   practice to do better.
C   try to ride other horses.
D   practice on a different saddle.

3. Juan lets out a deep sigh as he waits for the gate to open because he

    A   hopes he is ready.
    B   is hurt.
    C   wants to be finished.
    D   tries to remember what to do.

Use "Charros" to answer questions 4 - 7.

4. In paragraph 3, the word <u>competition</u> means

    A   act.
    B   contest.
    C   project.
    D   work.

---

5. How does David feel after he and his two friends finish the calf roping event?

    A   Frightened of the calf
    B   Surprised that he was ready
    C   Disappointed with his try
    D   Proud of his effort

6. Paragraph 7 is important because it helps the reader understand

    A   why Mexico has cowboys.

    B   why young cowboys learn to be charros.

    C   that charreadas take place to teach values.

    D   how many different skills are needed to be a charro.

---

7. The author provides information about the thoughts and feelings of which character in this story?

    A   David

    B   Juan

    C   Ricky

    D   Gerrado

Use "Second Best" and "Charros" to answer questions 8 - 9.

(Category 1 – 3 A – SS)

8. What is a common theme in both passages?

    A   Doing one's best
    B   Getting along with friends
    C   The care a family can show
    D   Sports are healthy

(Category 1 – Figure 19 F – RS)

9. Why are charreadas mentioned in both passages?

    A   To tell why the riders receive awards
    B   To show where the riders practice
    C   To explain the history of the riders
    D   To describe the roar of the crowds

67

Read the next two selections. Then answer the questions that follow them.

A LONG JOURNEY

<u>Characters</u> – Meg, Mick, Mom, Dad, Narrator

<u>Stage Set</u> – The backdrop shows a beach with an ocean, tall trees, and an illuminated half moon hanging above the stage. Sea turtles are scattered around the beach.

Scene 1

[Meg and Mick enter from stage left and run onto the center of the stage.]

1   **Meg**: *[shouting]* I see them! I see where the eggs are buried! They're making their way to the water! Hurry Mick! Help them get to the surf!

2   **Narrator**: Rushing about the dimly lit beach, Meg and her brother, Mick, set out to ensure that at least some of the baby green sea turtles will be able to cross the beach and escape past the coral reef into the deeper water of the ocean. Over many years, the constant wearing of waves upon the coral reef has formed a layer of sand creating a small beach at the edge of the island. Female sea turtles travel many miles and return to this coral atoll year after year to lay their eggs. Ten weeks later, baby sea turtles begin to hatch out of their nests in the sand.

3   **Narrator**: Meg and Mick's parents are scientists who travel to this island every summer to study tiny coral polyps that build the limestone coral reefs found scattered throughout the warm ocean waters near the equator. The twin brother and sister come with their parents and have developed a deep affection for the sea turtle families.

4   **Narrator**: A warm breeze blows through the tall trees and across the beach. A half moon faintly <u>illuminates</u> the life and death struggle of the baby turtles. Predators appear as the first of the turtles scamper across the sand toward the water.

5   **Meg**: *[Looking concerned]* Keep an eye out for birds. They are fast. Remember the last time? A flock of birds flew down from their nests and made off with a bunch of babies. If you make a lot of noise, you can scare them away and back into the trees. Maybe they will be too busy adding to their nests, chasing other birds, or fighting among themselves in the trees to notice this time. I'll keep watching for lizards and ghost crabs. They move fast but maybe I can thwart their attacks on the babies. We won't be able to save

all of the turtles, but we can help some of them get out to the open ocean.

6 **Narrator**: While Mick whoops, hollers, and waves his arms as he runs around the beach, Meg busies herself with using a long stick to push away any crabs, lizards, or other predators that attempt to grab the newly hatched sea turtles.

7 **Meg**: Mick, there's a bunch of turtles over by the waterline. Some birds are flying low on their way out to sea. [Shrieking] Get them! [Meg pounds her stick on the ground and rushes to the spot. She waves her free arm like she is chasing away a pesky fly.] Go away! Shoo! Leave these babies alone! They deserve a chance to live as much as you do!

8 **Narrator**: One sea bird swoops down and grabs a hapless turtle in its beak before Meg can chase it away. One last swing of the stick produces the desired result. The bird drops the baby sea turtle. It lands with a quiet splash in the rolling waves and promptly swims away.

9 **Meg**: [Crying out in delight] Yeah, keep swimming baby! Head on out to sea! Stay away from those groupers and sea eagles! Say hello to the equator for me!

10 **Narrator**: Meg turns around in time to see her brother running down a lizard in the middle of a small group of sea turtle hatchlings. Mick reaches down and manages to grab the lizard by its tail. With a flick of his wrist, he flings the startled lizard through the air into a clump of grass at the edge of the small beach. Shaking its head as if to clear the cobwebs, the lizard retreats to the safety of the thick underbrush.

11 **Narrator**: Mick hovers over the remaining baby turtles crawling toward the waves. He keeps a sharp watch for any ghost crabs that may pop out of the sand to grab one of the turtles. But within the blink of an eye, two turtles are snatched by a pair of ghost crabs that have buried themselves in the sand for just such an occasion. Mick spots a third crab before it is able to grasp onto the hind leg of one of the baby turtles with its claws and quickly scoots the turtle out of the way.

12 **Mick**: [Hollering] I think these guys are going to make it! They're in the surf and swimming over the reef. If the turtles can just make it into the deeper water on the other side of the coral reef, they should be in pretty good shape.

13 **Meg**: [Panting and out of breath] I hope you are right, Mick. Let's get home and rest up. I think tomorrow night will be better. Mom and Dad said they will join us. The more people here, the better

the chances the babies will make it out into the water and be able to start a new life in safety.

Scene 2

<u>Stage Set</u> – The backdrop shows a beach with an ocean, tall trees, and a bright sun is hanging above the stage. Sea turtles are scattered around the beach

[Meg, Mick, Mom, and Dad enter from stage left and run onto the center of the stage.]

14 **Meg**: *[Yelling]* Look at the baby turtles, Mom and Dad! They are heading out to sea!

15 **Mick**: *[Shouting]* Yes! They are doing what the others did yesterday. They are trying to get to the safety of the water!

16 **Mom**: Let's get busy helping keep them safe and free from predators that want to eat them for lunch!

17 **Dad**: Meg, you go over by the tree line and make sure that no animals get the baby turtles. Mick, you help me stay near the water and keep the crabs from attacking the baby turtles. Mom will stay in the middle and help out there.

18 **Meg**: *[Smiling broadly]* I think this is going to work!

CORAL REEFS

1   Coral reefs are underwater shelves or walls that dot the warm waters of Earth's tropical oceans just on either side of the equator. Created by the tiny coral polyps, these reefs are home to many fascinating plants and animals.

2   Coral polyps are very small creatures that use material found in ocean water to make a protective limestone barrier around the bottom half of their tiny bodies. The polyps can pull themselves down into these barriers and be protected from the harsh ocean that swirls around every minute of every day. Thousands and thousands of polyps live together making a coral reef. These polyps create other polyps and a new coral reef is born.

3   As polyps produce more polyps, the coral reef takes on its own unique shape, depending on the kind of coral it is. Some reefs look like they are made up of many big rocks while others grow like tree branches. Other coral reefs resemble the many antlers of a male deer. Still more reefs are flat and look like plates.

4   When coral polyps die the limestone stays behind. The coral reef continues to grow as the living polyps create new polyps. Coral reefs do not grow in an organized way, however. Shapes spread out all over. Various kinds of coral grow in and among each other. A tiny plant known as the coralline algae connects the different coral colonies together. These plants produce limestone, like the coral polyps, which binds all of the colonies into a coral reef.

5   Another tiny algae plant, called zooxanthellae, lives inside of the coral polyps. These plants and the polyps provide each other many of the materials each needs to live. Like all plants, the algae utilize light to make food. Coral reefs exist near the surface of the ocean, otherwise it is too deep for light from the sun to penetrate the water. Because of this, many coral reefs are located near land that rises above the waterline.

6   Fringing reefs grow like a shelf out into the ocean. They are connected to the land along the shoreline.

7   Barrier reefs are connected to the shore. They run parallel to it with areas of shallow water, called lagoons, separating the top parts of the reef from the shore.

8   A third type of coral reef is known as the coral atoll. A large inactive volcano that stops just short of the water's surface is completely surrounded by a coral reef. The coral reef sticks out above the water and is attached to the top of the volcano. A lagoon fills the space over the top of the volcano. Sometimes, the action of waves on the coral can <u>transform</u> the lagoon into an island. Plants

71

and trees begin to grow. Animals start to live there, too.

9   Many different kinds of animals live on or near coral reefs. Hundreds of different kinds of fish are found in the nearby waters. Snails, crabs, clams, sea stars, sea urchins, sea anemones, lobsters, oysters, sea turtles, and a variety of birds live in and around coral reefs.

10   Each organism contributes to and takes away from the coral community. It is this wide variety of creatures that makes coral reefs one of the most interesting environments above or below the oceans of the world.

Types of Coral Reefs

Fringing Reefs	Fringing reefs grow like a shelf out into the ocean. They are connected to land at the shore.
Barrier Reefs	Barrier reefs are parallel and connected to land at the shore. Some parts of barrier reefs are underwater.
Coral Atoll	Coral atolls are formed over an inactive volcano. A water-filled lagoon fills the center of the volcano. An island forms in place of the lagoon. • waves break up the coral reef • the pieces of coral reef are broken up into sand • the sand builds up over time and pushes out the water • the lagoon fills with sand • an island is formed

Use "A Long Journey" to answer questions 1 – 6.

(Category 1 – 2 A – RS)

1. What does the word <u>illuminates</u> mean in paragraph 4?

    A   Blows away
    B   Gathers among
    C   Lights up
    D   Passes by

(Category 2 – 6 A – RS)

2. Why does Meg tell Mick to watch out for birds along the beach?

    A   The birds may be chasing other birds away.
    B   The birds may be fighting among themselves in the trees.
    C   Meg knows the birds are wanting to add to their nests.
    D   Meg knows the birds had grabbed some turtles at an earlier time.

(Category 2 – 6 A – RS)

3. Why does Meg feel better about tomorrow?

    A   Her parents will help with the turtles.
    B   She knows where the turtle eggs are buried.
    C   Her brother will watch out for lizards and crabs.
    D   She remembers to tell her brother about the birds.

73

(Category 2 – 14 C – SS)

4. The picture is included in the selection to support the idea that sea turtles

    A   live in groups for safety.

    B   crawl across open beaches to lay eggs.

    C   are in danger from animals seeking turtle eggs.

    D   travel many miles to get to land.

(Category 2 – 5 – SS)

5. What can the reader conclude from the last paragraph of Scene 2?

    A   Baby sea turtles are hungry.

    B   The number of baby sea turtles are less than previous years.

    C   Baby sea turtles will make it to the safety of the water.

    D   The size of baby sea turtles has changed.

(Category 2 – 5 – SS)

6. Which sentence best summarizes Scene 2?

    A   Mom and Dad study the baby sea turtles.

    B   Meg and Mick try to get their parents to come and watch the sea turtles.

    C   Mom and Dad help Meg and Mick take care of baby sea turtles.

    D   Meg and Mick search for sea turtle eggs.

Use "Coral Reefs" to answer questions 7 – 10.

(Category 1 – 2 A – RS)

7. In paragraph 8, the word <u>transform</u> means

    A   build.

    B   change.

    C   cover.

    D   mix.

(Category 3 – 11 A – RS)

8. How does the information found in paragraph 4 help support the main idea of the passage?

    A   The information tells how coral reefs grow.

    B   The information explains how light affects coral reefs.

    C   The information describes the size of shapes found in coral reefs.

    D   The information shows that coral reefs are well organized.

(Category 3 – 13 B – SS)

9. What is the last step in the formation of a coral island?

    A   Waves break apart a reef's limestone.

    B   A reef surrounds an underwater volcano.

    C   Sand fills in a shallow lagoon.

    D   An underwater volcano stops being active.

(Category 3 – 10 A – SS)

10. The author probably wrote this passage to

   A   explain why people visit and study coral reefs.
   B   describe coral reefs and the ways they get started.
   C   explain where coral reefs are located around the world.
   D   describe the animals and plants found around coral reefs.

Use "The Long Journey" and "Coral Reefs" to answer questions 11 – 12.

(Category 1 – Figure 19 F – RS)

11. An idea present in both selections is

   A   ocean waves create sand from coral reefs.
   B   sea turtles travel many miles to lay their eggs.
   C   sea island birds feed on other animals for food.
   D   coral reefs are found in many shapes and sizes.

(Category 1 – Figure 19 F – RS)

12. Which topic does the author of each selection write about?

   A   The formation of a coral atoll
   B   The animals found on a coral atoll
   C   The measures scientists take to study creatures of the sea
   D   The struggle baby sea turtles endure to get to the deep waters of the sea

LEARN ABOUT YOUR BODY!

June 2011

BLOOD

Watchdog

1   A silent sentry guards you night and day, day in and day out. It defends you from outside invaders. Patrolling every corner of your body, it is ready to fight and protect you from anything that may threaten your health. This watchdog is your blood.

Through the Body

2   Flowing all through your body, this <u>vital</u> liquid keeps you alive. It carries necessary food and oxygen to every part of your body. This same blood also carries off the waste products that accumulate as your body lives, grows, and heals itself.

Body Cells

3   Your body is made up of very small cells. Each type of cell has its own special job to perform. To stay alive and healthy, these cells need food and oxygen. It is the blood that delivers the food and oxygen to the cells.

A Strong Muscle

4   The heart is a strong muscle that pumps the blood continuously through your body. It never tires. The heart beats and pumps blood every moment of your life. It is made up of two main parts. One side of the heart pushes the blood to the two lungs through tubes called "blood vessels." There the blood picks up fresh oxygen that you breathe in to take to the rest of the body. The blood returns to the other side of the heart and gets pumped out to all areas of your body.

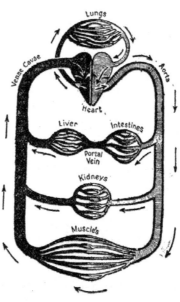

5   The blood leaves your heart through blood vessels called "arteries." These arteries branch out all over your body. As the arteries divide, they get smaller and smaller. Each cell in your body is connected to the

larger arteries by way of very tiny blood vessels called "capillaries." Blood travels one way through the capillaries. Food and oxygen from the blood passes through the short and extremely thin walls of the capillaries into each cell. The blood moves very slowly through the capillaries. On the other side of the capillaries are the "veins." These blood vessels take the blood back to the heart to be pumped once again to the lungs to receive life-sustaining food and oxygen. As the blood passes through the capillaries and releases food and oxygen, it also picks up the wastes produced by each cell as it does its own special job. Carbon dioxide is one of the waste products. The veins carry it back to the lungs and we exhale it.

Pumping Blood

6   Each time the heart beats, blood is pumped out through arteries and back through veins. As the heart relaxes between pumps, blood flows into the upper parts of the heart. These parts are called the "atria." Then the blood moves down into the bottom parts of the heart called the "ventricles." Special valves allow the blood to flow between the upper and lower parts of the heart. These valves prevent blood from going back and moving the wrong way. The blood in your body always circulates in the same direction. When the heart beats again, the blood in the ventricles gets squeezed out into the arteries. It is on its way to other parts of your body.

7   Valves in the arteries and the veins also prevent blood from going in the wrong direction. As the heart beats, the valves are opened, letting the blood flow freely. When the heart is between beats, these valves close, stopping any blood from flowing backwards.

Around and Around

8   The blood vessels throughout your body are in a special arrangement called the "circulatory system." The blood goes around and around, keeping your body healthy and on the go.

Made by the Bones

9   Blood is made by the main bones of your body. The insides of these bones contain "bone marrow." Here new blood cells are formed and enter the blood as it travels through vessels in the bones.

Blood Cells

10   Blood is a liquid made of different cells. They include red blood cells, white blood cells, and platelets. These cells float in the blood and are carried along as the blood moves through the body's veins and arteries. "Red blood cells" make up a large part of your blood. They carry oxygen from your lungs to the other cells in your body.

"White blood cells" are not nearly as numerous. They help clean the blood and protect your body from unwanted and harmful germs. "Platelets" are cells in your blood that help to stop your blood from bleeding outside of your body through cuts, scrapes, or scratches.

Stopping the Flow

11 When blood leaks from a vessel for whatever reason, your body is quick to react. Special chemicals are released into your blood causing the platelets to begin to bunch together. These bunches slow down the bleeding and even more bunches are formed. Rather quickly, the blood stops leaking and a scab is formed. The leak is fixed under the scab as the skin grows back together. The scab falls off when the healing process is finished.

A Remarkable Liquid

12 The blood in your body is a remarkable liquid. Each heartbeat pushes this fluid to every nook and cranny of your body keeping you healthy and alive.

My Notes About What I Am Reading

(Category 1 – 2 B – RS)

1. In paragraph 2, the word <u>vital</u> means

   A   complete.
   B   important.
   C   precious.
   D   special.

(Category 3 – 11 D – RS)

2. Which of the following would be helpful in finding information about bleeding?

   A   Through the Body
   B   A Strong Muscle
   C   Around and Around
   D   Stopping the Flow

79

(Category 3 – 11 A – RS)

3. This passage is mostly about

    A   why people bleed.

    B   how to give blood.

    C   the purposes of blood.

    D   why blood is mostly water.

(Category 3 – 13 B – SS)

4. The picture included in this selection helps the reader understand

    A   that harmful germs are cleaned by the blood in the body.

    B   that blood travels in one direction through the body.

    C   how quickly bleeding stops when blood leaks from the body.

    D   how blood is made by the bones of the body.

(Category 3 – 11 A – RS)

5. Read the outline of information in paragraph 5.

    > 1.   Why the capillaries work so well
    >
    > **A** Thin walls
    > **B** Next to the cells
    > **C** Carry food to the cells
    > **D** _____

    Which information belongs in the blank?

    A   Short vessels

    B   Blood moves slowly

    C   Blood travels in one direction

    D   Blood travels with each heartbeat

(Category 3 – Figure 19 D – RS)

6. Which of these sentences from the passage shows the reader that the heart is always working?

    A   *The heart beats and pumps blood every moment of your life.*

    B   *One side of the heart pushes the blood out through tubes called "blood vessels" to the two lungs.*

    C   *Each time the heart beats, blood is pumped out through arteries and back through veins.*

    D   *As the heart beats, the valves are opened letting the blood flow freely.*

(Category 3 – Figure 19 E – RS)

7. Which is the best summary of the passage?

    A   Blood is made in the human body by the bones. Brand new blood cells are formed and sent into the rest of the body through the many blood vessels that run all over. Some of the cells are called red blood cells. These cells take oxygen from the lungs to other parts of the body to help with repairs and growth. Other cells are called white and these cells help keep the blood clean while helping get rid of germs that have entered the body. A third group of cells called platelets help stop blood from bleeding once there has been a cut, scrape, or scratch.

    B   The heart is a strong muscle in the body that pushes the blood from one place to another. The heart is always beating so the blood is always   moving. Blood passes through the heart and leaves in blood vessels called arteries. The blood goes to parts of the body and returns through blood vessels called veins. Blood only is able to go one way on its trip around the body.

    C   The human body contains the liquid, blood, which helps keep people alive. The heart pumps blood through tubes called blood vessels to all parts of the body. The blood carries food and oxygen that the cells of the body use to repair themselves and grow. The blood also picks up wastes made by the cells and helps the body get rid of them. Bones make the red and white cells found in blood. These cells carry the food and oxygen and protect the body from germs.

    D   The human body is made up of cells. Cells are hard workers because they help the body repair itself and grow. The blood carries many of these cells to all parts of the body through the blood vessels that travel through the heart and lungs. Once the blood has picked up oxygen and food, it makes its way to the various parts of the body ready to provide what is needed for the body to get better if hurt and stay healthy. Oxygen enters the body and goes into the lungs where it passes to the blood. The body needs oxygen to stay alive.

FULL OF ENERGY BARS

1   With the Full of Energy Bar you get an energy boost, great taste, and low calories. Each bar is also low in fat and high in fiber. Now you can enjoy a great tasting snack bar without having to worry about climbing on a scale. The Full of Energy Bar will provide a quick and easy way to keep weight off. You won't have to make an appointment with your dentist to have your teeth checked. Each and every Full of Energy Bar is full of vitamins and nutrients your body needs to be healthy and stay healthy. Many other snack bars are full of sugar and fat. Not so with the Full of Energy Bars. No other snack bar comes close to the quality of the Full of Energy Bars.

2   The Full of Energy Snack Company has been providing healthy and nutritious snacks for over thirty years. Its founders started the company with one snack: The Original Full of Energy Chips, made from potato slices. Now there are twenty-five snack foods with the introduction of the Full of Energy Bar.

3   The Full of Energy Bar comes in four delicious flavors. There is strawberry, apple, grape, and raspberry. Each bar includes bits of chocolate, rice, vitamins, nutrients, and a special sauce that holds everything together. The customers that buy our bars tell us it is the sauce that tastes so wonderful. Each batch of the sauce is checked by our top taste specialists. It is this sauce that has been in every one of our snacks since the very first one was made.

4   In actual taste trials, every nine out of ten people preferred our Full of Energy Bar over four other leading snack bars. When many of these tasters found out it was the Full of Energy Bar, they couldn't believe their choice. Here are some of the comments made by the tasters.

5   *"The Full of Energy Bar is the best snack bar out on the market today. Full of Energy Bars should be in every student's lunch bag. My Full of Energy Bar was gone is three bites." Juan – Chicago*

6   *"Full of Energy Snacks have been in stores since I was eight years old. I think they taste really good with milk." Millie – New York*

7   *"Even the wrapper on the Full of Energy Bar is inviting. The Full of Energy Bar sells for seventy-five cents. At that price, I will always love to buy the bar."* Dave – Boston

8   *"My friends are going to love the Full of Energy Bars. Each one has 100 calories and 1 gram of fat."* Mary – San Francisco

9   Each and every Full of Energy Bar goes through a rigorous cooking process. Care is taken to make sure each bar is made fresh and upholds the standards of quality that have kept Full of Energy Snack Company one of the top companies in its field. If you ever have problems with any of our snack foods or are not completely satisfied, please let us know. We will <u>promptly</u> re-fund your purchase price. You will not have to wait long. We want to help you in any way we can so our courteous staff is eager to make you happy.

My Notes About What I Am Reading

(Category 1 – 2 A – RS)

1.   What does the word <u>promptly</u> mean in paragraph 9?

   A   Carefully
   B   Cleanly
   C   In a quick manner
   D   With little doubt

(Category 3 – 11 B – SS)

2.   Which sentence from the passage represents a fact?

   A   *"The Full of Energy Bar is the best snack bar out on the market today."*
   B   *"Full of Energy Snacks have been in stores since I was eight years old."*
   C   *"Even the wrapper on the Full of Energy Bar is inviting."*
   D   *"My friends are going to love the Full of Energy Bars."*

(Category 3 – 12 A – SS)

3. The author compares the Full of Energy Bars to

   A   cereal.

   B   other snack bars.

   C   fruit.

   D   potato chips.

(Category 3 – 11 B – SS)

4. Which sentence from the passage represents a fact?

   A   *"I think they taste really good with milk."*

   B   *"At that price, I will always love to buy the bar."*

   C   *"Each one has 100 calories and 1 gram of fat."*

   D   *"Full of Energy Bars should be in every student's lunch bag."*

(Category 3 – 12 B – SS)

5. Which statement by the author seems to be an exaggeration of the facts in the passage?

   A   *If you ever have problems with any of our snack foods or are not completely satisfied, please let us know.*

   B   *Now there are twenty-five snack foods with the introduction of the Full of Energy Bar.*

   C   *In actual taste trials, every nine out of ten people preferred our Full of Energy Bar over four other leading snack bars.*

   D   *No other snack bar comes close to the quality of the Full of Energy Bars.*

(Category 3 – 12 A – SS)

6. The author organizes the information in this passage mostly by

    A   stating what the Full of Energy bar is made of and providing satisfied customers' comments.
    B   comparing the Full Energy Bar to other energy bars on the market.
    C   describing problems with energy bars and offering solutions.
    D   listing ways energy bars can help people get healthy.

(Category 3 – 12 B – SS)

7. Which statement by the author from the passage seems to be misleading?

    A   *The Full of Energy Snack Company has been providing healthy and nutritious snacks for over thirty years.*
    B   *Each bar is also low in fat and high in fiber.*
    C   *The Full of Energy Bar will provide a quick and easy way to keep weight off.*
    D   *The Full of Energy Bar comes in four delicious flavors.*

(Category 3 – 14 C – SS)

8. The picture next to paragraph 3 is included with the passage most likely to show the

    A   care taken in preparing the sauce.
    B   reason the company uses sauce in the bar.
    C   ingredients used in the bar's sauce.
    D   flavors available for the sauce from the company.

(Category 3 – 14 C – SS)

9. The author provides the picture next to paragraph 7 to

   A   show the reader how often the customer eats a bar.
   B   let the reader know how the customer feels about the bar.
   C   let the reader see where the customer can get the bar.
   D   describe to the reader what happens to the customer once a bar is eaten.

(Category 3 – Figure 19 D – SS)

10. The reader can tell that the snack company wants

   A   to make new products.
   B   to have a lot of money.
   C   many people on staff.
   D   satisfied customers.

11. Read the first sentence of a summary of the passage.

Summary

The Full of Energy Bar is full of healthy ingredients. _____
_____

Which set of sentences best completes the summary?

A   People like to eat the Full of Energy Bar. Customers from all over the country are happy with the food. Someone ins San Francisco says that the bar has only ten calories.

B   The Full of Energy Bar comes in strawberry, apple, grape, and raspberry flavors. Each bar has many vitamins and nutrients. A special sauce is put in every bar. This sauce has been in all of the Full of Energy Snack Company products.

C   The Full of Energy Snack Company makes many healthy snacks including the full of Energy Bar which comes in four flavors. Each bar is full of vitamins, fiber, and a special sauce. Many customers are happy with the snack bar. The Full of Energy Snack Company is available to help its customers.

D   Snack bars can provide energy to people. The Full of Energy Bar can help people stay out of the doctor's or dentist's office. The bars can be bought in stores all over the country. One customer was able to buy the bar for seventy-five cents.

Read the selection *"Two Ways to Get Healthy!"* before answering the questions below.

TWO WAYS TO GET HEALTHY!

1   In just minutes a day, you will make all of your friends jealous. Instead of getting winded from just walking down the street, you will be able to run in long distance races and hardly break a sweat. Imagine feeling and looking better. With our amazing product, you will feel and look better.

2   Our fantastic product will help take and keep weight off. Your muscles will get bigger and stronger with each workout. After working with our product, you will hardly be able to recognize yourself. The changes in your health will be unbelievable. Friends and even your family will not believe it is you. The changes will be that dramatic.

3   What is this great product? It is called the "Jump-It Rope". The "Jump-It Rope" is like a jump rope but even better. You can get your very own "Jump-It Rope" in one of eight colors and four lengths. The "Jump-It Rope" comes in blue, green, red, yellow, orange, brown, black, and purple. It comes in lengths of five feet, seven feet, nine or eleven feet. The five foot length is popular for individual jumpers. The other lengths are often used by groups of jumpers working together to get in shape.

4   As with any exercise program, it is important that you are examined by a doctor. Once you are considered fit to start to exercise, our "Jump-It Rope" comes with a choice of at least four programs designed to improve your health. The first one starts you slowly and gradually, carefully increasing the amount of exercise you get each time you use the program. The second one is similar to the first but it increases the amount of exercise you receive at twice the speed of the first program. The third program is like the first and second but increases the exercise speed at three times the first program. The fourth program is designed strictly to improve your heart.

5   If you follow these programs consistently, you will begin to experience results right away. Muscles will grow bigger and stronger, weight will drop off, inches will start to fall away, and you will be able to be on the go for longer periods of time before you feel tired.

6   If you like our "Jump-It Rope" you will like our "Heavy Bar". This piece of equipment will allow you to improve the health of your heart. The hollow metal bar comes in only one color: black. With

88

this <u>solitary</u> product, you will also be amazed at the health benefits available to you. This single piece of equipment is designed to be used by only one person at a time. You can put it on the floor and jump back and forth to either side. The bar can be held in your hands 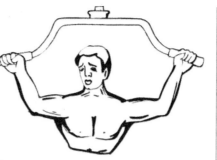 and you can run in place. Two extra bonus features of the "Heavy Bar" are the two exercise programs that come with it on a DVD. The two thirty minute workouts on the DVD will help keep you motivated and keep track of your progress as you use the bar every day of the week. Regular exercise is key to being and staying healthy.

7   Which ever product you decide to purchase, please tell your friends and neighbors of the great changes you experience in your health. They make great gifts. You may also go online and visit our website to see more. Write, call, or email us and let us know, too. For more information or to place an order, call 1-800-555-2087.

<table>
<tr><td>My Notes About What I Am Reading</td></tr>
</table>

(Category 3 – 11 C – RS)

1.   Look at this diagram of information from the selection.

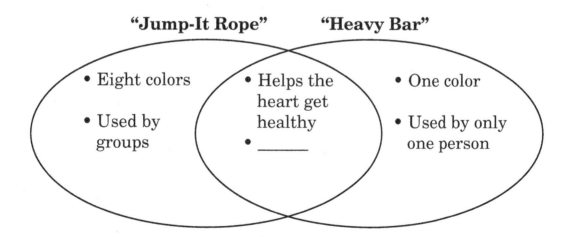

"Jump-It Rope"   **"Heavy Bar"**

- Eight colors
- Used by groups

- Helps the heart get healthy
- _____

- One color
- Used by only one person

Which of these belongs on the blank line?

A   Used by doctors

B   Used for jumping

C   Comes in only one length

D   Comes with one exercise program

(Category 1 – 2 B – RS)

2. In paragraph 6, the word <u>solitary</u> means

    A   single.
    B   large.
    C   new.
    D   quiet.

(Category 3 – 12 A – SS)

3. According to the author of this Passage, if the reader uses the "Jump-It Rope",

    A   better fitness will be the result.
    B   friends will visit more often.
    C   doctor visits will be less often.
    D   exercise equipment will be easier to use.

(Category 3 – 11 B – SS)

4. Which sentence from the selection represents a fact?

    A   *With our amazing product, you will feel and look better.*
    B   *In just minutes a day, you will make all of your friends jealous.*
    C   *For more information or to place an order, call 1-800-555-2087.*
    D   *If you like our "Jump-It Rope" you will like our "Heavy Bar".*

(Category 3 – 12 B – SS)

5. Which statement from the passage by the author is misleading?

   A   *The five foot length is popular for individual jumpers.*

   B   *Friends and even your family will not believe it is you.*

   C   *You can get your very own "Jump-It Rope" in one of eight colors and four lengths.*

   D   *As with any exercise program, it is important that you are examined by a doctor.*

(Category 3 – 12 A – SS)

6. How does the author organize the passage?

   A   By listing ways the products are able to improve people's health

   B   By comparing one person's experiences with exercising to another person's experiences

   C   By describing the two products and explaining how they help people get in shape

   D   By stating the author's opinions about exercising and then providing evidence to dispute them

---

(Category 3 – 12 B – SS)

7. Which statement from the passage is an exaggeration?

   A   *The "Jump-It Rope" comes in blue, green, red, yellow, orange, brown, black, and purple.*

   B   *The other lengths are often used by groups of jumpers working together to get in shape.*

   C   *This single piece of equipment is designed to be used by only one person at a time.*

   D   *After working with our product, you will hardly be able to recognize yourself.*

91

(Category 3 – 14 C – SS)

8. The author most likely uses the picture next to paragraph 1 to let the reader know that

    A   having the jump rope is expensive.
    B   using the jump rope will change the way you feel.
    C   using the jump rope is a lot of work.
    D   having the jump rope takes you away from other activities.

(Category 3 – 14 C – SS)

9. The picture next to paragraph 6 is used to show

    A   how the bar makes exercising easy.
    B   why the bar makes a great gift.
    C   why the bar is all in one piece.
    D   how the bar is able to be used by one person.

(Category 3 – Figure 19 D – SS)

10. From information provided in the passage, the reader can tell that

    A   exercising is better when done with friends.
    B   products can be found less expensive in stores.
    C   customers can purchase additional products.
    D   customers like to do more than one exercise program at a time.

11. Which is the best summary of the passage?

    A   The "Jump-It Rope" and the "Heavy Bar" can help people get and stay in shape. The "Jump-It Rope" comes in different lengths and colors. The "Heavy Bar" is designed for one person. Each product can be used in various exercise programs.

    B   The "Jump-It Rope" is used by people to get healthy. It is a jump rope that can be used by one person or a group of people. Before starting any exercise program, it is best to be examined by a doctor.

    C   The "Heavy Bar" is a product that can be used to help people exercise the heart. It is hollow and comes in black. The bar can be placed on the floor or held above the head while exercising.

    D   The "Jump-It Rope" and the "Heavy Bar" come with exercise programs. These programs are used to help the heart get stronger. If you use these products you will look different. Your family will not be able to recognize you.

Read the selections "A Cool Wind" and "Out of Nowhere" before answering the questions below.

A COOL WIND

1 It is soft and light on my uplifted cheeks.
   When the heat comes from the sun.
   It picks up dust and whirls it around,
   Like rapid racers recklessly on the run.
   Shoooooo! Shoooooo!

6 When clouds are dark and threatening,
   It's mighty as mighty can be.
   It can lift the roof off of a house.
   And uproot a tall elm tree.
   Shoooooo! Shoooooo!

11 It carefully lifts a colorful kite.
   High into the sky.
   It can hold a feather <u>suspended</u> in the air.
   With a hot and hefty, "Hi!"
   Shoooooo! Shoooooo!

16 The wind is surely invisible.
   It is very hard to see.
   But, like that dust, I'll float on the wind,
   As it roams all wild and free.
   Shoooooo! Shoooooo!

94

OUT OF NOWHERE

1   "I'm getting dust in my eyes!" shouted Melissa. "Help me, Pete!"

2   "Quick, close your eyes and stand perfectly still," replied Pete. He rushed up to his friend while she covered her eyes with her hands. Pete took hold of Melissa's arms to stop her from running. As the wind moved on, the dust and leaves that had been swirling around Melissa continued on their journey across the open field next to her house.

3   Using the ends of her fingers to gently wipe the tears from her eyes, Melissa said, "I didn't even see it coming. One minute everything was quiet and calm. The very next minute I was surrounded by this whirl of leaves and dust. What happened?"

4   "You were caught in a wind whirl," said Pete. "Since you cannot see it, a wind whirl can sneak up on you seemingly out of nowhere. That is what just happened to you. Wind can go just about anywhere on Earth. It is that free. The best thing is to just stay still and let it pass. Oh yes, and keep your eyes closed."

5   "Thank you," said Melissa with a smile. "Next time I'll do just that."

Use "A Cool Wind" to answer questions 1 – 7 below.

(Category 1 – 2 B – RS)

1. Read this line from the poem.

    It can hold a feather <u>suspended</u> in the air.

    What does the word <u>suspended</u> mean as it is used in the poem?

    A   Backing
    B   Hanging
    C   Gathering
    D   Forming

2. Which line from the poem best shows the sound made by the wind?

    A   It picks up dust and whirls it around,
    B   The wind is surely invisible.
    C   But, like that dust, I'll float on the wind,
    D   Shoooooo! Shoooooo!

---

3. Read this line from the poem.

    > **Like spiders on the run.**

    What does the phrase mean in the poem?

    A   The dust moves quickly.
    B   The dust is heavy.
    C   The dust is scary.
    D   The dust moves quietly.

---

4. From information provided in the poem, the reader can tell that the author

    A   is afraid of the wind.
    B   enjoys being around wind.
    C   has little experience with wind.
    D   likes sharing the wind with friends.

(Category 2 – 14 C – SS)

5.   The picture lets the reader know that the wind

    A   is able to change the way people feel.

    B   helps people with chores.

    C   blows all the time.

    D   can move things around.

(Category 2 – 4 A – SS)

6.   Read the line from the poem.

> **Like rapid racers recklessly on the run.**

The author uses these words to

    A   describe the speed of the wind.

    B   show the reader the force of the wind.

    C   explain the amount of damage done by the wind.

    D   tell the reader the location of the wind.

97

7. Read the first sentence of a summary of the poem.

Summary

Wind is caused by heat from the sun. _____

_____

Which set of sentences best completes the summary?

A   Wind can be strong enough to hurt things. It can blow the roof off of a building. The wind can lift a tree out of the ground. Dark clouds may show up when the wind is strong.

B   Wind is something that cannot be seen. It is invisible but still can move things. Sometimes the wind is light enough to move feathers. The wind can also move kites.

C   Wind can move things around. Sometimes it is very strong and damaging. Other times it is light and careful. The wind cannot be seen as it moves on its way.

D   Wind is able to blow on people's faces. It moves across their cheeks. The wind is able to move quickly. It sometimes makes dust and leaves go from place to place.

Use "A Cool Wind" and "Out of Nowhere" to answer question 8.

(Category 1 – 3 A – SS)

8. Which theme is present in both passages?

A   The wind is strong and powerful.

B   The wind is able to go where it wants.

C   The wind is caused by the sun.

D   The wind can be used by people.

98

Read the selections "Clowns" and "Already Tired" before answering the questions below.

CLOWNS

1 My eyes are wide and my mouth a grin.
   I see the views as the show begins.

3 The tent grows dim while one light shines.
   Three rings all around in a staggered line.

5 A parade comes out to excite the crowd.
   While the ringmaster sings and shouts aloud.

7 The clowns start first, they're my favorite part.
   They tell us now that the show will start.

9 White faces painted with merry grins.
   Their <u>antics</u> take the whole crowd in.

11 Clowns jump and spin and fall right down,
   They seek a laugh, a grin, but no frown.

11 Clowns jump and prance with long dark shoes.
   They're big brown boats with toes as crews.

13 Clowns throw treats into the air.
   And pails of paper hug my hair.

15 The pranksters move with leaps and bounds.
   I love the madcap circus clowns.

ALREADY TIRED

1 "Hurry, Murray, the show is about to start!" shouted Freddie. "You don't even

   have your bright pink wig on your head. When are you going to get your huge shoes on your feet? Let's go!"

2 "I'm sorry, Freddie," said Murray. "I've been a bit slow getting started today. I have been practicing all morning on the new act. I do so want everyone to like it and laugh so hard that they begin to cry."

3 "Me too, Murray," grinned Freddie. "That's why I do what I do. It makes my heart soar like an eagle every time someone in the au-

99

dience laughs at one of our skits, stunts, pranks, or jokes. But we won't be able to do or see any of that if you don't get a move on. Here, let me help."

4   Freddie grabbed Murray's wig and plopped it down on Murray's head. It

wobbled into place and settled there like a cap eraser on the end of a pencil. Then, grabbing each of the huge plastic shoes, Freddie worked with Murray to fit each foot into its proper shoe.

5   After the second shoe was resting snugly on his right foot, Murray said, "Whew! I am already tired. Getting ready to make people laugh can sure be hard work!"

Use "Clowns" to answer questions 1 – 5 below.

(Category 1 – 2 B – RS)

1.   What does the word <u>antics</u> mean in line 10?

  A   Funny acts
  B   Wild stories
  C   Crazy pictures
  D   Exciting people

(Category 2 – 4 A – SS)

2.   Read this line from the poem.

> **They're big brown boats with toes as crews.**

The author uses these words to

  A   tell what the clowns do to get people to laugh.
  B   explain how the clowns are able to move around.
  C   describe what the clowns have on their feet.
  D   show how the clowns practice their tricks.

100

(Category 2 – Figure 19 E – SS)

3. Which is the best summary of the passage?

    A   There are three rings inside of a tent. A ringmaster talks to the crowd. The crowd watches to see what is going to happen next.

    B   A group of clowns throws treats into the air. They throw paper into the air, too. The clowns have big feet.

    C   A show starts inside of a tent. A group of clowns leads a parade and tells the people watching what the show is going to be about. The clowns move around and get the crowd to laugh.

    D   People are sitting in seats inside of a tent and they are watching a ringmaster. The people are all laughing at clowns. Someone throws treats into the air along with paper.

(Category 2 – 8 A – RS)

4. The phrase "They're big brown boats with toes as crews." is important to the passage because it

    A   describes who is wearing the shoes.

    B   shows the size of the clowns' shoes.

    C   explains where the clowns got their shoes.

    D   tells what the shoes sound like.

101

5. Which set of rhyming lines from the poem help the reader understand how clowns get their audience to laugh?

    A   *My eyes are wide and my mouth a grin.*
        I see the views as the show begins.

    B   *The tent grows dim while one light shines.*
        Three rings all around in a staggered line.

    C   *A parade comes out to excite the crowd.*
        While the ringmaster sings and shouts aloud.

    D   *White faces painted with merry grins.*
        Their antics take the whole crowd in.

Use "Clowns" and "Already Tired" to answer question 6.

(Category 1 – 3 A – SS)

6. Which theme is present in both passages?

    A   Clowns want to lead the show.

    B   Clowns want to be on time.

    C   Clowns try to get people to laugh.

    D   Clowns try to learn new things all the time.

102

Read the selection "Sun" before answering the questions below.

SUN

1   Long ago, a small planet started on a long journey to find a place to call home. He wanted to be far away from his family, the nearby stars. The planet searched and searched for a spot where he could live as he wanted. After years of having others watch over him, he longed to care for himself.

2   With time, the planet found what he was looking for. As the lights of his family flickered in the far off distance, the planet settled in to his new home. He looked forward to living on his own.

3   The small planet soon fell asleep. Shortly after, he awoke with a shiver. His landscape was cold. The planet saw that his streams, lakes, and rivers were as solid as a brick wall. Even the oceans were beginning to turn to ice.

4   "My outside needs heat," said the small planet. "My insides will help."

5   Without hesitating, the small planet made volcanoes <u>erupt</u> all over. He gathered the hot lava and formed a huge ball. The small planet threw the ball into the nearby heavens. Soon the streams, lakes, and rivers were flowing again. The oceans tossed and turned as usual. The small planet was warmed by the glowing ball now called the sun.

(Category 2 – 3 B – SS)

1. What event is explained by this myth?

    A   How the sun came to be
    B   Why there is water
    C   Why planets are cold
    D   How the stars flicker

103

(Category 1 – 2 B – RS)

2. What does <u>erupt</u> mean in paragraph 5?

    A   To break apart

    B   To become hard

    C   To fall away

    D   To burst forth

(Category 2 – 8 A – RS)

3. The author uses the phrase "as solid as a brick wall" in paragraph 3 to

    A   explain where water comes from.

    B   show how water is clear.

    C   describe what the water looks like.

    D   tell why water is on the earth.

(Category 2 – Figure 19 D – SS)

4. From information found in the passage, the reader can tell that the small planet

    A   grew tired of being around his family.

    B   needed to be taken care of by someone.

    C   wanted to take a vacation.

    D   felt disappointed with his search for a new home.

104

Read the selection "Friends for Mars" before answering the questions below.

FRIENDS FOR MARS

1   Mars was sad. He looked around at everyone else. Earth laughed as Saturn told a funny story. Mercury and Venus played hide-and-seek. Jupiter read a book to Uranus. Mars thought everyone else seemed to be enjoying their life. Mars moaned and sighed. He did not know why he was not happy.

2   Aunt Neptune approached Mars. "What is wrong?" she inquired. "Why are you so sad?"

3   "I am not sure, Aunt Neptune," answered Mars. "I look at every one else having fun. They all seem as happy as a child in a candy store."

4   Aunt Neptune looked at the other planets. She looked at Mars. Aunt Neptune smiled.

5   "I think I know why you are unhappy," said Aunt Neptune. "I may be able to help."

6   "How can you help me?" asked Mars.

7   "Go back to your home," said Aunt Neptune. "I will send someone to you. Just wait and you will be sad no more."

8   Mars returned to his home. He waited as his Aunt Neptune had said. A few days later, Mars noticed as two small moons sauntered up to him.

9   "Hello," said the two moons together. "Aunt Neptune sent us to come and visit you. She said that you were not happy and needed friends. Can we stay here with you and be your friends?"

10 Mars was overwhelmed. He did not know what to say. Finally, he managed to nod up and done and say with a huge smile, "Yes, please stay and be my friends. My aunt was right. I am quite jubilant."

(Category 2 – 3 B – SS)

1. What event is explained by this myth?

   A   What made the rings of Saturn
   B   Why Mercury is a planet
   C   How Mars got two moons
   D   Where the planets come from

(Category 1 – 2 B – RS)

2. The word <u>jubilant</u> in paragraph 10 means

   A   annoyed.
   B   joyful.
   C   anxious.
   D   surprised.

(Category 2 – 8 A – RS)

3. Why does the author use the phrase "as a child in a candy store" in the selection?

   A   To describe what the planets like to do for laughs
   B   To show how the planets feel about their friends
   C   To explain why the planets are arranged in a certain way
   D   To tell where the planets are found

106

(Category 2 – Figure 19 E – RS)

4. Which is the best summary of the passage?

    A   Mars is unhappy, but does not know why. Mars' Aunt Neptune finds out why Mars is unhappy. She sends two friends to help. Mars becomes happy.

    B   Mars is not happy. Aunt Neptune comes to visit. Mars tells her why he is not happy. Aunt Neptune understands.

    C   Mars sees other planets playing. They are having a good time. They all have friends. Mars does not have any friends.

    D   Mars wants to be happy. She is not happy. Two moons come to visit Mars. The two moons talk to Mars.

(Category 2 – 6 C – SS)

5. Who is telling the story?

    A   Earth

    B   Moon

    C   Saturn

    D   Another character not in the story

Read this selection. Then answer the questions that follow it.

COWBOY BREAKFAST

1   "Yee-hah! Yip-yip-yip-yahoo! Time to get out of bed because there is a lot to do to get the cowboy breakfast up, running, and ready!" shouted Wrangler Dave.

2   Four sleepy campers poked their tousled heads out of two separate tents. The two in the first tent rubbed their eyes and shook themselves awake.

3   "Hey, Wrangler Dave," said the more awake of the pair. "What's going on? It's dark outside. I'm still tired and sore from riding horses and rounding up stray calves from yesterday. Please wake me up when the sun says it's about 10:30."

4   The other tent dweller joined in, "Yeah, me too. You got us up so early, the stars just went to bed."

5   The two campers in the second tent finally managed to rouse themselves sufficiently awake and offered something to the conversation.

6   "Brianna, we have to get up and get going. We volunteered to help with the breakfast. Remember?" said a red-haired freckle-faced boy.

7   "And it was your idea, too," added a tall lanky youngster, also a boy.

8   "I didn't think it would be that hard to fix some eggs and a little hot chocolate. We didn't expect it to be quite so early, either," complained Maxine, the other girl in the first tent. "The stars are still out and the sun isn't up yet, either."

9   Grabbing a pot in one hand and a wooden spoon in the other, Wrangler Dave banged them together. "Let's go campers! In just a short time you are going to have a bunch of hungry people wondering where their cowboy breakfast is. We can't just improvise this operation. It takes a significant amount of working ahead of time and teamwork. You, as volunteer cooks, are on the clock!"

10 All four scrambled out of their tents, pulled on some warm outer clothes, and gathered around Wrangler Dave's chuck wagon.

11 "You'll be able to clean up after breakfast, since I let you sleep a little later than I should have," said Wrangler Dave. "Now, here's our menu this morning: cowboy scrambled eggs, pork sausage, skillet gravy, irresistible buttermilk biscuits, fresh fruit, and hot chocolate."

108

12 "Do the cooks get to eat first?" asked Maxine.

13 Wrangler Dave turned and gave Maxine a long look and then grinned, "The cooks get to eat after everyone else has been served, but there's no harm in tasting while you cook."

14 Maxine seemed to busy herself wiping some dust off of her shoes. "I'll guess I'll eat when everyone else is finished," she replied.

15 "My regular crew has started the camp fires. Most of the egg mix and biscuit batter has been made ready. Brianna you will help with the eggs, Maxine the biscuits, Ian the sausage, and Terrell the gravy," explained Wrangler Dave.

16 The volunteer cooks set to work. Four fires set up by Dave's crew blazed next to the chuck wagon. Thick logs burned in each rock-rimmed circular campfire. Tangled piles of wood sat to the side. Black metal poles pointed straight up on the outside rim of rocks around each fire. One crackling fire had a rod holding a simmering pot of water resting across the vertical poles. Wire grills holding thick skillets stretched across two of the fires. Sausage sizzled in one and eggs and gravy cooked over the other. Deep Dutch ovens rested in the remaining fire. Coals heaped on the top of each oven glowed red as buttermilk biscuits baked inside. Aromas mingled together drawing any observers closer for a better look.

17 Dave's busy crew showed the four cooks what they needed to do. Brianna stirred the eggs. Maxine added biscuits to empty Dutch ovens and set them in the fire. She used a small shovel to pile burning coals on the lids of the ovens. Ian checked and turned browning sausage patties while Terrell stirred thick bubbling gravy.

18 Off to the east, pink and orange streaks of light told of the coming dawn. Ian stopped and looked up.

19 "Wow, what a view! Hey, Terrell, look above the far canyon wall," said Ian. "The sun is coming up. It's beautiful!"

20 Terrell paused his stirring and looked. "You're right, Ian. The colors are a lot sharper here than in the city."

21 "Keep stirring, Terrell," urged Wrangler Dave. "You don't want to burn the gravy. I'll wake you up tomorrow morning and you can see the sun come up while another team prepares the breakfast."

22 As each fire died down, more wood was added and soon strong bright flames licked the underside of skillets full of the hearty breakfast foods. Each volunteer cook moved around the fires like a bee in a hive.

23 "I can feel muscles I did not know I had because of this situation,"

My Notes About What I Am Reading

said Maxine as she spooned biscuits into a big pot to keep them warm. "I'm glad we didn't ask to help with lunch and supper, too."

24 Wrangler Dave banged a spoon against a pot one more time. "I'm as pleased as a crow at a June bug convention. You all have done a <u>superb</u> job of helping get our cowboy breakfast ready. It all looks great. In about five minutes, the rest of the camp will be getting up and heading this way. As soon as you serve them and they finish their breakfast, you may eat. Then, take a while, relax, enjoy the beautiful scenery, and help my crew wash, dry, and put away all of the breakfast equipment."

25 "I'll be glad when tomorrow comes," said Ian. "I will get to sleep in."

26 "Oh no," countered Terrell. "You're getting up with me to see the sun come up and do more horseback riding around the ranch to look for lost cows before we go home on the day after tomorrow."

<table>
<tr><td>**My Notes About What I Am Reading**</td></tr>
</table>

(Category 1 – 2 A – RS)

1. In paragraph 9, the word <u>improvise</u> means to not

    A   fix.

    B   keep track of results.

    C   do one's best.

    D   plan.

(Category 2 – 6 B – RS)

2. Which sentence from the selection shows that Maxine realizes fixing breakfast at camp is hard work?

    A   *"Do the cooks get to eat first?"*

    B   *"I'll guess I'll eat when everyone else is finished,"*

    C   *"I can feel muscles I did not know I had because of this situation,"*

    D   *"The stars are still out and the sun isn't up yet, either."*

(Category 2 – 8 A – RS)

3. In paragraph 9, what does Wrangler Dave mean when he says the four cooks are "on the clock"?

    A   They are working.

    B   They are wasting time.

    C   They are almost finished.

    D   They are ready to get started.

(Category 1 – 2 B – RS)

4. What does the word <u>superb</u> mean in paragraph 24?

    A   Just so

    B   Very good

    C   Nearly complete

    D   Extremely popular

(Category 2 – 6 A – RS)

5. What is Terrell going to do the next day?

    A   Go home

    B   Wash dishes

    C   Cook dinner

    D   Get up early

6. The reader can tell from this story that life as a member of Wrangler Dave's cooking crew is

    A   relaxing.
    B   difficult.
    C   solemn.
    D   ordinary.

---

7. Which sentence from the selection best shows that Wrangler Dave is organized?

    A   *"Time to get out of bed because there is a lot to do to get the cowboy breakfast up, running, and ready!"*
    B   *"You don't want to burn the gravy."*
    C   *"In about five minutes, the rest of the camp will be getting up and heading this way."*
    D   *"It all looks great."*

---

8. The author's use of figurative language in paragraph 24 emphasizes that

    A   Wrangler Dave is happy with the breakfast workers.
    B   Wrangler Dave feels surprised at how the breakfast turned out.
    C   Wrangler Dave becomes aware of what the campers did at breakfast.
    D   Wrangler Dave decides to try another approach to complete breakfast.

Read the selection "A Different Point of View" before answering the questions below.

A DIFFERENT POINT OF VIEW

1 Georgia O'Keeffe was an amazing artist. Her paintings of everyday simple objects were colorful and lively. The shapes and colors she used emphasized the smallest details in the objects she painted. They gave notice to things that were often overlooked.

2 Georgia painted many pictures of things found in nature. She portrayed flowers, mountains, shells, and animal bones. She would often make her paintings larger than life. Her attention to usually ignored details of commonplace things set her paintings apart from other artists. Strong vivid colors <u>enhanced</u> the shapes and designs of what she chose to paint.

3 Born on a farm in Wisconsin in 1887, Georgia spent a lot of time learning about nature. Her parents allowed her to have art lessons while she was growing up. They encouraged Georgia to study art after high school. She studied art in schools in Virginia, Chicago, Illinois, and New York City. Georgia did well in her studies and improved her skills. Even at an early age, Georgia showed an unusual ability of looking at the world around her in a different way.

4 Georgia decided to become an art instructor after teaching a class at one of the schools she had attended. She was a good teacher and enjoyed working with young people. Georgia took a job in Texas teaching art. The wide open spaces of Texas appealed to her. She began to show her enjoyment in the paintings she created. Paintings of the sky and the desert displayed the beauty she saw in this colorful landscape.

5 After a while Georgia returned to New York City. There she began to paint with bold bright colors. Many of her paintings were of flowers. The paintings were large and showed flowers close up. She made the viewer feel and experience even the smallest detail.

6 People began to take notice of her paintings. There were not very many women artists in the 1920s. More and more people came to see Georgia's work. They were struck by her choice of objects to paint and by the original style she presented. Her paintings looked different than the works of other artists.

7 Each painting that Georgia crafted was special to her. She worked hard on each one and had a difficult time letting go of them. Soon, her paintings were selling for thousands of dollars.

8   In the mid-1920s, Georgia traveled away from New York City to visit New Mexico. There she noticed and painted the clear skies, tall mountains, and the many colors of the desert. Georgia was also <u>drawn</u> to paint desert flowers, hills, rocks, and animal bones she found scattered about New Mexico. She liked this place so much that she decided to move and live there permanently. Georgia lived and painted in New Mexico for most of the rest of her life.

9   In her later years, Georgia became involved in her community. She helped many people and donated money to improve her town. In 1986, Georgia O'Keeffe died at the age of ninety-eight. Her special paintings continue to provide beauty and enjoyment to people throughout the world.

My Notes About What I Am Reading

(Category 1 – 2 B – RS)

1. In paragraph 2, the word <u>enhanced</u> means

    A   taken apart.

    B   brought about.

    C   made even better.

    D   shown the way.

(Category 1 – 2 E – RS)

2. Read the meanings below for the word <u>drawn</u>.

    > **drawn** (drôn) *verb*
    > **1.** moved toward
    > **2.** received **3.** stretched
    > **4.** figured out

    Which meaning best fits the way <u>drawn</u> is used in paragraph 8?

    A   Meaning 1

    B   Meaning 2

    C   Meaning 3

    D   Meaning 4

114

(Category 2 – 7 A – SS)

3. Look at this chart of information.

Georgia O'Keefe
Painted things in nature
Studied art in Chicago
Lived in New Mexico

Which of these belongs in the empty box?

A   Painted people

B   Created small paintings

C   Encouraged by her parents.

D   Used vague colors.

(Category 2 – Figure 19 D – SS)

4. Which sentence from the passage shows that Georgia O'Keeffe painted things differently?

A   *She worked hard on each one and had a difficult time letting go of them.*

B   *Her special paintings continue to provide beauty and enjoyment to people throughout the world.*

C   *Her paintings of everyday simple objects were colorful and lively.*

D   *Her attention to usually ignored details of commonplace things set her paintings apart from other artists.*

(Category 2 – Figure 19 D – SS)

5. With which statement would the author most likely agree?

A   Georgia O'Keeffe successfully attempted to show the beauty of nature in her paintings.

B   Georgia O'Keeffe was comfortable painting like other artists of her day.

C   Paintings showing things in nature are more beautiful than paintings of people.

D   Paintings showing nature are hard to make look like the real thing.

Read this selection. Then answer the questions that follow it.

SPORTS NEWS

News from the World of Sports

August 2012   *Issue 4, Vol. 6*

Table Tennis
by L. Jackson

1   "Ping! Pong!"

2   "Pong! Ping!"

3   If you do not know that sound, you must not be a table tennis player. Table tennis is sometimes referred to as ping-pong because of the "ping" sound made when the racket, or bat, hits the ball and the sound of "pong" made when the ball hits the table.

History

4   Table tennis has its roots in England from the game of lawn tennis. Begun in the late nineteenth century, table tennis was played indoors on dining room tables. It was called a variety of names including "Whiff-Whaff", Gossimar", and the more well known "Ping-Pong". The first patent for table tennis was awarded in the 1890s. Celluloid balls were introduced from the United States in the early 1900s. Prior to that, balls had been made of cork or rubber. Early bats were made of wood with animal skins stretched over them. Modern bats are still made of wood, but are covered with a layer of sponge and then a top layer of rubber. The addition of pimpled or studded rubber enabled the players to put a spin on the ball. This gave more speed and movement to the ball as it traveled back and forth across the court.

5   The game became very popular. Table tennis tournaments were organized in the early 1900s and prize money was awarded to the winners. Table tennis associations sprang up all around the world in the 1920s. The first world championship was held in 1927. The International Table Tennis Federation (ITTF) was established. The United States founded its own association and joined the ITTF.

6   Modern tournaments are made up of many different matches with players from all around the world. Men, women, boys, and girls from under ten years old to participants past seventy-five years of age compete alone or in teams of two, or doubles. In 1988, table tennis became an Olympic event. Players from China, Japan, Sweden, Hungary, and South Korea have often dominated world championship tournaments.

| My Notes About What I Am Reading |

Important Dates in the History of Table Tennis

1891 – The first patent for table tennis is awarded

1901 – Table tennis tournaments are started in many countries

1902 – The country of Japan learns about table tennis

1926 – The International Table Tennis Federation is formed

1933 – The United States forms its own table tennis association and joins the ITTF

Equipment

7 Table tennis uses some basic equipment: a bat, balls, and a table. Serious players also invest in clothing and shoes that help them play their best.

8 The bat is used to hit the ball. Most players choose one that rests comfortably in their hands. Balls are white and hollow. Ones are preferred that have a consistent bounce and last a long time. The wooden table ranges in size from nine feet long by five feet wide by two and a half feet high. The table is usually a green color with a six inch high net strung across the middle from one long side to the other. A white stripe runs down the length of the center but is used only in doubles play.

Rules

9 Table tennis involves hitting the ball back and forth over a net. Play continues until one of the players misses hitting the ball, hits the ball into the net, knocks the ball off of the table, or bounces the ball more than once or not at all on his or her side of the net before sending it to the other player.

10 Play begins when one player serves the ball to the other. The serving player holds the ball in the flat palm of one hand. The ball is tossed into the air and struck as it falls and before it hits the table. The ball must bounce on the server's side of the table before going over the net and bouncing on the other player's side or court. This player then must hit the ball with the bat causing it to bounce once first on his or her side, sail over the net, and bounce once on the opposing player's side. Play continues in this fashion until an error is made. If a serve touches the net on its way over, it is played again. Serving is done by the same player until five points have been scored.

11 A player receives a point when the other player makes an error. A game is won by the first person to achieve twenty-one points. If the score is tied at 20 each, the game continues until one of the players

wins with a two point lead. Matches consist of two or three games. The first player to win two games is the winner of the match.

12 During play and after a serve, if the ball hits the net or the edge of the table, it is a good shot. If the ball hits the side of the table, it is not a good shot and the one who hit the ball loses the point.

13 Table tennis games with teams of two players, or doubles, are a little bit different. The serve must go from the right hand court and land in the other players' right hand court. The players must hit every other shot. Players shift positions every time the serve changes. A player serves to the other player at the start of a new game. If the game is the deciding one, table ends are changed and players on the same team switch places when either team reaches ten points.

Tips

14 Here are a few tips to help you become a better player.

1. Take the time to warm up. Spend a few minutes running in place and doing jumping jacks. This will get the heart pumping. Your muscles will be ready for the match.

2. Practice making your serves all look the same. Your skill will improve the more time you spend on it. A serve with little or no spin on the ball should look the same as a serve with lots of spin. Your opponent will not be able to tell what kind of ball will be served if each serve looks the same.

3. Mix up your serves. Make them move at different speeds and land on different areas of the court.

4. Also mix up your return shots. Have some land close to the net and make others land near the middle or end of the table on the other side of the net. Alternate the return from one side to the other. Always keep the other player guessing. Make sure the <u>encounters</u> with your opponent are immediate and quick.

5. You need to play to the other player's weaknesses and stay away from the strengths. This would seem to make sense, but always keep it in mind.

6. Above all, have fun!

(Category 1 – 2 E – RS)

1. Read the definition below for the word <u>encounter</u>.

encounter (en koun' tər) *verb*   **1.** to come in contact with   **2.** to meet in conflict unexpectedly

noun   **1.** a direct meeting   **2.** an unexpected meeting

Which definition best fits the way <u>encounters</u> is used in paragraph 14?

A   Definition 1 - verb
B   Definition 2 - verb
C   Definition 1 - noun
D   Definition 2 - noun

(Category 3 – 11 A – RS)

2. The author includes information in paragraph 8 to help the reader understand

A   Where table tennis is played
B   How table tennis is set up
C   Things used to play table tennis
D   What makes a good ball in table tennis

(Category 3 – 13 A – SS)

3. What is the first activity a player should do when getting ready for a game of table tennis?

A   Get the heart pumping
B   Practice different kinds of serves
C   Find out the other player's weaknesses
D   Learn to put a spin on the ball

(Category 3 – 10 A – SS)

4. What is the author's purpose in this article?

    A   To persuade readers to play a popular game
    B   To tell readers about a popular world-wide game
    C   To describe to readers why table tennis is so popular
    D   To explain to readers where table tennis got its name

---

(Category 3 – 12 A – SS)

5. The author of the article would most likely agree that

    A   table tennis is an easy game to play.
    B   table tennis can be mastered by anyone.
    C   expensive equipment will help players win games.
    D   the more a player learns about the game, the better the play.

(Category 3 – 11 B – SS)

6. Which sentence from the article expresses an opinion?

    A   *This will get the heart pumping.*
    B   *Always keep the other player guessing.*
    C   *Table tennis involves hitting the ball back and forth over a net.*
    D   *Table tennis games with teams of two players, or doubles, are a little bit different.*

(Category 3 – Figure 19 D – SS)

7. Which sentence from the article supports the idea that the more you practice the better you will be at playing table tennis?

    A   *Your skill will improve the more time you spend on it.*

    B   *Alternate the return from one side to the other.*

    C   *Make them move at different speeds and land on different areas of the court.*

    D   *You need to play to the other player's weaknesses and stay away from the strengths.*

(Category 3 – 13 B – SS)

8. The chart is included in the selection to support which idea?

    A   Table tennis is a team sport.

    B   Table tennis is a world-wide sport.

    C   Table tennis involves skill and conditioning.

    D   Table tennis affects the cultures of a variety of countries.

(Category 3 – 11 D – RS)

9. In which section of the passage does the author include information that supports the idea of winners and losers?

    A   History

    B   Equipment

    C   Rules

    D   Tips

(Category 3 – Figure 19 E – RS)

10. Which is the best summary of the selection?

    A   Table tennis is an indoor game that has its roots in England and is now played the world over. Participants use a paddle to bat a small ball over a low net stretched across the middle of a wooden table. Players must let the ball bounce only once on their side of the net before sending it back over the net to the opposing player's side. Points are awarded to one player when the other makes an error, with the winner declared at twenty-one points. Practice and attention to serves and return shots help players perform better.

    B   Table tennis is an Olympic sport played by many people in countries all around the world. The game was invented more than one hundred years ago. Single players or pairs of players battle each other using paddles to hit a ball over a net on a wooden table. The people of Japan are familiar with the game as well as the people in the United States. An international association with many members has been in existence for many years.

    C   The game of table tennis is sometimes known as ping-pong. Players hit a ball over a net and try to win points from opposing participants. Better players practice their serves to attempt to make them difficult to return properly. Other players try to make all of their shots look the same to confuse their opponents. The more a player practices, the better the player becomes.

    D   The game of table tennis has many rules to help players keep track of the game. Participants try to be the first to reach a score of twenty-one points to win a game. Players keep a small ball in play on a wooden playing surface while attempting to cause opponents to make errors. If a ball bounces more than one time on a player's surface, a point is awarded to the player causing the error. Table tennis is a fun game.

(Category 3 – 14 C – SS)

11. The illustration is included to support which idea?

    A   Table tennis can be easy to learn.
    B   Table tennis can be fun to play.
    C   Table tennis has many rules to help players keep track of the game.
    D   Table tennis has taken a long time to be accepted by players.

Read the selections "A Special Treasure" and "A Homemade Checkerboard" before answering the questions below.

A SPECIAL TREASURE

1   <u>Characters</u> – Narrator, Mr. Tyler, Mrs. Tyler, Daniel, Rose

2   <u>Stage Set</u> – The backdrop shows the inside of a small cabin. Mrs. Tyler sits in a rocking chair off to the side. Rose is reading a book off to the other side. Mr. Tyler and Daniel are sitting across from each other at a small table in the center of the room.

3   *[Daniel and Mr. Tyler are playing checkers.]*

4   **Mrs. Tyler**: *[weaving a basket with reeds]* I think we should plant more wheat come spring, what do you think, Henry?

5   **Narrator**: Mr. Tyler rests his chin on his hands, pondering his next move.

6   **Daniel**: Come on, Papa. You've been sitting there for almost five minutes.

7   **Mr. Tyler**: Uh, yes, Martha, I think we should plant more wheat next spring. *[glancing up at Daniel]* Hold your horses, Daniel. Just give me time. I think I have a move here that will work just fine for me.

8   **Narrator**: Mr. Tyler rests his chin on his hands and waits for a moment. Then he pushes one of his three remaining red checkers slowly into an adjoining black square, careful to keep his index finger resting on the checker. Silently, he takes one last search over the board and, with a confident smile, talks to Daniel.

9   **Mr. Tyler**: Your move, Daniel.

10 **Daniel**: It sure is, Papa!

11 **Narrator**: Before his father can blink twice, Daniel grabs one of his black checkers and quickly jumps all three of the red checkers.

12 **Daniel**: That's the game, Papa!

13 **Mr. Tyler**: What? How did you do that?

14 **Rose**: *[snickering]* That's three in a row, Papa.

15 **Narrator**: Mr. Tyler looks down at the few black checkers resting on the tray at the end of his side of the wooden checkerboard. He runs his rough and calloused fingers gently across the old checkerboard, worn smooth from hundreds of games. Lingering over

123

seven faint yellow stars positioned next to a white crescent moon on the tray at one end of the board he speaks.

16 **Mr. Tyler:** I remember the first time I won three games in a row from my father. He couldn't believe it either. This board has sure seen its share of games. My grandfather made it when he was eleven years old with his father's help. A few of the checkers have been lost over the years, but we replaced them with new wooden ones. I hope you too grow to love the game and <u>cherish</u> the memories this old board brings as much as I do. It has meant a lot to me.

17 **Rose:** We will, Papa. We do.

18 **Mr. Tyler:** [*wiping his eyes with his shirt sleeve*] Charlotte, why don't we celebrate Daniel's victories with some of that delicious apple pie.

A HOMEMADE CHECKERBOARD

1 Checkers has been a favorite board game for many years. Many generations of families have spent quiet evenings next to a fire as a rain or snow storm howls outside, playing games of checkers while sitting comfortably indoors. You too can <u>allay</u> the hustle and bustle of everyday living with a relaxing game of checkers on your own handmade checkerboard.

2 Years ago, people made their own checker games. They took great care in constructing a board decorated with pictures or designs. These checkerboards were then handed down from family member to family member. Young children were taught how to play the game by parents or other relatives in the family. Families often enjoyed an entire evening playing checkers.

3 You can easily make your own checkerboard with just a few simple materials. A couple of extra minutes spent creating and adding your own pictures or designs will make the board special for you.

4 **Materials:**
two or three big pieces of newspaper
a piece of sixteen-by-twenty-four-inch heavy cardboard
a ruler
a pencil
red and black markers
a box of crayons
twenty-eight two-inch round wooden chips
a self-seal plastic bag

124

5   Directions:

1. Open up two or three big pieces of newspaper and put them on an open table. Set the cardboard on the newspaper.

2. Draw a straight line across both narrow ends of the cardboard with the ruler and pencil. Make the lines four inches from each end. This four-inch space at each end of the board will be the tray. This is where players put their opponents' checkers after they have jumped over them.

3. Put dots, using the pencil and ruler, every two inches along each of the four sides of the large center square on the checkerboard.

4. Use the ruler and the pencil to connect the dots from one side across to the other. When you have finished, there will be a playing surface of sixty-four squares, each two inches wide.

5. Start at one corner and color in every other square with a black marker all the way across the row. Then use a red marker and color in the squares in between the black ones all the way across the row.

6. Go on to the next row. Start off by coloring every other square with a red marker. Use a black marker to color in the squares in between the red ones in this row all the way across. If done properly, you will have alternating squares of red and black (or black and red) all of the way across each row.

7. Use the crayons to draw and color any pictures or designs that you want in the tray at each end of the board. Some examples are pictures of the moon and stars, rainbows, clouds, trees and mountains, animals, or family members.

8. Count out fourteen of the two-inch round wooden chips and color both sides red with a marker. Count out fourteen more chips and color them black on both sides. This will give you two extra checkers of each color. Use the plastic bag to store the red and black wooden checkers.

9. Once you have finished making your checkers and the checkerboard, you must find a partner and enjoy a couple of games of checkers.

Use "A Special Treasure" to answer questions 1 through 7.

(Category 1 – 2 B – RS)

1. In paragraph 16, the word <u>cherish</u> means

    A look over.

    B hold dear.

    C keep ready.

    D take care.

(Category 2 – 8 A – RS)

2. In paragraph 7, Mr. Tyler tells Daniel to "hold his horses" because he wants Daniel to

    A leave.

    B move.

    C rest.

    D wait.

(Category 2 – 6 B – RS)

3. How does Mr. Tyler feel after Daniel wins three checker games in a row?

    A Angry

    B Foolish

    C Nervous

    D Surprised

(Category 2 – 6 A – RS)

4. Paragraph 15 is important because it helps the reader understand

    A   that Mr. Tyler is a good checker player.
    B   why Mr. Tyler put pictures on the checkerboard.
    C   how Mr. Tyler feels about the checker game.
    D   why Mr. Tyler made the checker game.

(Category 2 – 5 – SS)

5. Which of these events shows a change in Dad's character in the play?

    A   Dad agrees to plant wheat in the spring.
    B   Daniel wants to play checkers.
    C   Daniel wins three checker games in a row.
    D   Dad thinks it is time to eat pie.

(Category 2 – 5 – SS)

6. What can the reader conclude from the last paragraph of the play?

    A   Dad is fond of the memories of his checkerboard.
    B   Dad has a hard time believing the age of his son Daniel.
    C   Dad wants to get right to work on planting the wheat.
    D   Dad thinks it is time to learn to play a new game.

7. The author uses the picture next to paragraph 4 to let the reader know

   A   how to play checkers.
   B   Mr. Tyler is thinking about his next checker move.
   C   which checkers to move next.
   D   Mr. Tyler wants to get the board ready for the next game.

Use "A Homemade Checkerboard" to answer the questions 8 through 10.

8. In paragraph 1, the word <u>allay</u> means

   A   arrange.
   B   bless.
   C   calm.
   D   enjoy.

---

9. What happens before dots are connected with lines on the checkerboard?

   A   A red marker is used to color in squares.
   B   Crayons are used to draw pictures on the checkerboard.
   C   Twenty-eight wooden chips are counted out.
   D   Pieces of newspaper are opened.

(Category 3 – 10 A – SS)

10. The author probably wrote this passage to

    A   persuade the reader to play easy games.

    B   inform the reader about why people play games.

    C   give the reader rules about a special game.

    D   explain to the reader how to make a popular game.

Use "A Special Treasure" and "A Homemade Checkerboard" to answer questions 11 and 12.

(Category 3 – 11 E – RS)

11. One way these passages are alike is that both mention the

    A   reasons people play checkers.

    B   steps used to play games.

    C   supplies needed to construct a familiar game.

    D   pictures that are on the ends of a checkerboard.

(Category 1 – Figure 19 F – RS)

12. An idea present in both passages is

    A   families playing checkers over many years.

    B   the materials used to make a checkerboard.

    C   the steps followed in making a game.

    D   families working inside in the evening.

Read the selection "Flowers" before answering the questions below.

FLOWERS

1   Years ago, the flowers on Earth were able to move along the ground. They liked to go from place to place and not stay too long in one spot. The flowers were always mischievous. They liked to play tricks on other plants and animals.

2   One day, a group of flowers decided to play a trick on a hive of bees. The bees were trying to get pollen to make honey. They used the flowers. The flowers kept moving away from the bees. Just when the bees would arrive at the flowers, the flowers would rush away to a different spot. After several hours, the bees grew tired and pleaded with the flowers to stay still. The flowers just laughed and scampered away to a new spot. This left the bees without any pollen to make into honey.

3   The bees were upset. They buzzed off to Mother Nature's home in the forest. They asked to see Mother Nature. She met with the bees. The bees told Mother Nature all that the flowers had done.

4   Mother Nature sat and listened. She tried to <u>console</u> the bees. She was quite concerned because other groups of animals had come to her about the problems caused by the flowers. Mother Nature thought long and hard before she made a decision. The flowers would stay in one spot. No longer would they be able to move around on their own. Roots would go into the ground to soak up food and water. The flowers would spend all of their lives in one place.

(Category 2 – 3 B – SS)

1.   What event does this myth explain?

   A   How flowers got leaves
   B   Why flowers stay in one place
   C   Why flowers make seeds
   D   How flowers smell

130

(Category 1 – 2 E – RS)

2. Read the meanings for the word <u>console</u>.

> **console** (kən sōl') *verb* **1.** To comfort
> (kän' sōl) *noun* **1.** The part of an organ that holds the keys **2.** A
> cabinet that holds a radio or TV **3.** A raised part between car seats

Which meaning best fits the way <u>console</u> is used in paragraph 4?

A   Meaning 1 - verb
B   Meaning 1 - noun
C   Meaning 2 - noun
D   Meaning 3 – noun

(Category 2 – 6 A – RS)

3. Paragraph 1 is important to the passage because it

A   explains how the flowers act.
B   describes what the flowers look like.
C   shows where the flowers live.
D   tells who likes the flowers.

(Category 2 – 6 C – SS)

4. Who is telling this myth?

A   Flowers
B   Mother Nature
C   Bees
D   Another character not in the myth

CPSIA information can be obtained at www.ICGtesting.com
Printed in the USA
BVOW10s1053030316

438922BV00016B/50/P